How To READ & UNDERSTAND EDUCATIONAL RESEARCH

Sara Miller McCune founded SAGE Publishing in 1965 to support the dissemination of usable knowledge and educate a global community. SAGE publishes more than 1000 journals and over 800 new books each year, spanning a wide range of subject areas. Our growing selection of library products includes archives, data, case studies and video. SAGE remains majority owned by our founder and after her lifetime will become owned by a charitable trust that secures the company's continued independence.

Los Angeles | London | New Delhi | Singapore | Washington DC | Melbourne

How To **READ &**
UNDERSTAND
EDUCATIONAL
RESEARCH

James Williams

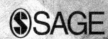

Los Angeles | London | New Delhi
Singapore | Washington DC | Melbourne

Los Angeles | London | New Delhi
Singapore | Washington DC | Melbourne

SAGE Publications Ltd
1 Oliver's Yard
55 City Road
London EC1Y 1SP

SAGE Publications Inc.
2455 Teller Road
Thousand Oaks, California 91320

SAGE Publications India Pvt Ltd
B 1/I 1 Mohan Cooperative Industrial Area
Mathura Road
New Delhi 110 044

SAGE Publications Asia-Pacific Pte Ltd
3 Church Street
#10-04 Samsung Hub
Singapore 049483

© James Williams 2020

First published 2020

Apart from any fair dealing for the purposes of research or private study, or criticism or review, as permitted under the Copyright, Designs and Patents Act, 1988, this publication may be reproduced, stored or transmitted in any form, or by any means, only with the prior permission in writing of the publishers, or in the case of reprographic reproduction, in accordance with the terms of licences issued by the Copyright Licensing Agency. Enquiries concerning reproduction outside those terms should be sent to the publishers.

Editor: James Clark
Assistant editor: Diana Alves
Production editor: Nicola Carrier
Copyeditor: Audrey Scriven
Proofreader: Leigh C. Smithson
Indexer: Silvia Benvenuto
Marketing manager: Lorna Patkai
Cover design: Naomi Robinson
Typeset by: C&M Digitals (P) Ltd, Chennai, India
Printed in the UK

Library of Congress Control Number: 2019948055

British Library Cataloguing in Publication data

A catalogue record for this book is available from the British Library

ISBN 978-1-5264-5925-1
ISBN 978-1-5264-5926-8 (pbk)

At SAGE we take sustainability seriously. Most of our products are printed in the UK using responsibly sourced papers and boards. When we print overseas we ensure sustainable papers are used as measured by the PREPS grading system. We undertake an annual audit to monitor our sustainability.

Table of Contents

About the Author

Dr James Williams is a Senior Lecturer in Education in the School of Education and Social Work at the University of Sussex. James initially studied geology at the University of London and subsequently trained as a science teacher. He taught secondary science in North London (Enfield), South London (Croydon) and Surrey. He has been involved in initial teacher education and training for over 20 years and teaches on various undergraduate and postgraduate education programmes.

His research interests currently entail understanding the place and teaching of 'The Nature of Science' and 'The Scientific Method' in the school curriculum, in particular, what teachers understand about these concepts and ideas. Linked to this work he also researches the teaching of evolution in science and the place of creationism in a school-based context. He has published a number of successful textbooks on science for Key Stage 3 children, as well as authoring articles in international education journals and a book on teaching the nature of science.

Acknowledgements

I would like to thank my wife, Joan, for her unfailing support during the writing of this book. As a colleague she provided help and advice, as a partner she put up with numerous evenings and weekends of me tip-tapping on a keyboard.

I am indebted to my colleague Professor Kwame Akyeampong for coining the phrase 'what carries on working', which has been used within the book at various points. As he states, implementing a change that 'works' can be relatively easy to do and record. Whether or not it continues to work is another matter. Ultimately, this is what education research should seek to accomplish – not just what works, but what continues to work long after the research has finished.

I am also indebted to various colleagues at Sussex who read early drafts of chapters. Their feedback, either written or in person, has helped shape the final book. Their encouragement confirmed that I was on the right track.

Finally I would like to say thank you to my editors at SAGE, in particular Diana Alves, who enthusiastically supported the project from the word go and provided very helpful feedback on and corrections to the various drafts of the chapters.

Introduction

My own journey in education research has been long and, at times, a bumpy one. The word 'research' means many different things to people. Look at the numerous synonyms for research (such as 'investigate', 'conduct investigations into', 'study', 'inquire into', 'probe', 'analyse', 'examine', 'explore' etc.) and it is easy to think we know what research is, but as with all academic disciplines 'the devil is in the detail' as they say. This book is about that 'detail'; it is about demystifying the culture and practice of research. It looks at the exacting nature of research and how we describe and interpret research.

My personal research journey

My initial track in life was science. I studied geology, specialising in evolutionary palaeontology. The rules for research in the sciences are very different (though there are many similarities) from those applied in the social sciences. The first ever 'research' I carried out was mapping geological formations in North Wales and Northern Ireland. This was more a training in techniques than trying to uncover or find some new explanation for something. My undergraduate dissertation – 'The Ecology of Jurassic Dinosaurs' – was labelled as a research dissertation, though it was distinctly descriptive rather than analytical. It was, for an undergraduate dissertation, what I would now see as nothing special, just acceptable.

My Master's dissertation, this time in science education, was historical. It focused on the life and work of Alfred Russel Wallace, a Department of Science and Arts (DSA) examiner and former 'teacher', who was most famous for the co-discovery of the theory of evolution by means of natural selection with Charles Darwin. Looking back on this, it was, again, also more descriptive than analytical, though it did reveal some lesser known facts about his life and work. Each time I undertook research I was refining skills and learning techniques. Researchers do this all the time – it is a lifelong learning process.

My foray into genuine educational research meant developing a new set of skills and a very different way of thinking from those I had developed as a scientist and amateur historian of science. The truth is, I struggled to move from a scientific mindset to that of a social scientist. For example, I was very dismissive and critical of small datasets.

Case studies were 'interesting' but did nothing to help us really understand what was going on. Like some researchers in education today, I was wedded to the idea of things like large datasets that are generally representative of the population. More recently, randomised controlled trials and methods that replicate what scientists do are gaining in popularity. The aim, we are told, is to uncover 'truths' about education in the same way that we uncover explanations for natural phenomena in science (it is worth pointing out here that science does not aim to deliver 'truth'; the best it can do is deliver explanations that fit the known evidence). I came to understand that both small- and large-scale studies, randomised controlled trials and less well-controlled 'interventions' all have a place in finding out what works and, more importantly, what continues to work in education.

I am now acclimatised to education research, to the ways in which different researchers approach problems to find solutions and/or explanations. I still have an intuitive feeling for larger studies, producing empirical data that are representative of the population being studied, using methods whereby the researcher is on the outside looking in. At the same time, my experiences have led me to understand better how humans are very complex beings. The variables we encounter in education, when trying to research teaching and teachers, learners and learning, mean that the creation of universal methods or approaches to teaching is unlikely to happen. For all those traditional teachers who reject child-centred learning and discovery-based, or problem-based, learning as faulty, problematic and unsuccessful, there are teachers who can make such methods succeed. Likewise, progressive teachers dismissive of colleagues who use direct instruction and rote learning, who extol the virtues of the 'knowledge-based curriculum', can be shown plenty of examples where such approaches are successful. If we are going to have one universal 'truth' in education, for me it would be that there is no one best way to design a curriculum, plan a lesson, deliver teaching or assess children. With this in mind, reading and interpreting education research is about locating the findings on a continuum or series of continua. The skill of the teacher is in selecting which point on each continuum is appropriate for the children, the subject, the context within which they find themselves.

Why a book on how to read and understand educational research?

This book is the sort of book that, as a novice researcher in education, I would have liked to have read before I embarked on serious research – indeed before I started reading research. My early reading of education research papers was filled with incredulity and misunderstanding. Not knowing 'how' education research was done and what the terms meant that I came across, I dismissed certain ideas as 'nonsense'. For example, there is only one reality – surely? The idea of multiple realities in social science research was, to me, nonsense. However, is it any different from what science proposes – the multiverse? That there are parallel universes that contain multiple versions of us all living parallel, yet different, lives in alternate realities?

I was confronted by many different research 'paradigms': post-positivism; post-feminism; post-structuralism; post-realism; critical realism etc. So many 'posts' I felt I could almost build a fence. Then there were the various ways in which you could investigate reality. It was all very confusing. When you add to this the language of social science research (and here I acknowledge that all research fields, including science, have their own particular and specialist language), frankly it was all just a bit too much. Epistemology, ontology, axiology, phenomenology, hermeneutics … I could go on. I really needed someone to demystify the language and simply tell me what I needed to know in order to get to grips with research, and to understand better how to read and interpret academic research. This is where this book begins – it is the basic premise for it. It is about demystifying, making simple and laying out all the things I wish I had been told at the start of my education research journey.

There are many books that will tell you *how* to do research – what methods to use, how to construct good questionnaires, how to conduct statistical analysis of empirical data. Many of these books will also have glossaries which have definitions of some of those polysyllabic conundrums I slipped into the text a few lines earlier. What is often absent from such books about 'how' to do research is the deconstruction of meaning. What this book provides are simple explanations (rather than just definitions) for the words that appear incomprehensible, and descriptions of the various methods and paradigms commonly used in education research. For example, a short and to-the- point explanation of what 'critical realism' is or what epistemology really means in the context of education research – that and so much more.

Research can be a bit of a car crash

My initial reading of academic research many years ago was, in all honesty, a bit of a car crash. That set me thinking. A car crash is a great analogy for explaining some of the core concepts of education research, and this analogy is explained further below.

RESEARCHING A CAR CRASH

Three central terms that everybody reading and doing education research quickly becomes aware of are 'epistemology', 'ontology' and 'axiology'. These are not everyday words that are generally understood. Explaining what they are and how they apply to research is one of the first jobs of any research supervisor. My preferred way of achieving this is to use a 'car crash' analogy.

(Continued)

Imagine you come across a car accident at a busy roundabout in a town. A white van has driven into the side of a saloon car. There are witnesses, there are police in attendance and other emergency vehicles and workers. People are standing around, others are looking busy – a forensic traffic officer has a measuring tape and is taking photographs. The research question here is 'What happened?', and it's a simple question.

The problem is that finding out what happened is not always straightforward. Ask any police officer and they will tell you that even though 10 people may all have witnessed the same event, you will never have one 'true' description. The witnesses will all construct their own realities of what has happened: each person will deliver what they think is the truth and they will even be able to justify their 'belief' using evidence. Others who may not have seen the accident will have opinions based on what they can see now: they will try to reconstruct what happened using past experience and any evidence they have in front of them.

Perhaps two people saw the accident from one viewpoint, while another person was on the opposite side of the roundabout and witnessed the same accident, but from a very different viewpoint. The police, who were not there when the accident occurred, are charged with finding out 'what happened'. The lead officer will be, in effect, the lead researcher. How does she go about this? She needs to have a 'research paradigm'. In this instance we are going to say that she will use 'critical realism' – put simply, this means that she believes a reality exists (the accident happened), and what she needs to do is investigate scientifically what happened, but also understand that in science not everything can be known. We must apply a critical eye to the evidence we collect and acknowledge that some accounts of the 'event' will differ.

The lead researcher – the lead investigator of the accident – will perform a set series of actions that have been devised and well-rehearsed – the research method. Putting to one side the police procedures, the officer is likely to ask the following: How do we know what happened and how can we investigate what we know? They will also have a set of values and ethics related to how they should proceed. These three things are analogous to epistemology, ontology and axiology.

Epistemology is about the nature of knowledge and things such as belief, opinion, truth and justification. In our accident scenario, what do the witnesses believe happened? Is their account justified in any way? Are they all telling the truth? What if there was a passenger in the car? Is the passenger telling the truth when they say, 'the van came out of nowhere, really fast'? In gathering 'data' our researcher will be trying to understand the nature of the knowledge they have. Is what the passenger says biased? Or independent? Ontology is about how we investigate reality or 'being'. The forensics team will be investigating the reality of the accident. They will be taking measurements, finding skid marks, looking at the distances and trying to calculate the speed the vehicles were travelling at. They will look at the road surface, the weather conditions and any factors that could influence what happened. They may even try some experiments to test the road conditions, for example driving a 'control' vehicle fitted with cameras and sensors along the stretch of road to test the condition of the surface. Ontologically, our investigating officer is examining the reality of the crash and trying to establish 'the truth'.

Axiology is about values and the nature of those values. Witnesses to the accident may be biased – they may, for example, see a white van and invoke a stereotype that all white van drivers are a menace. As a result, the witness statement of the passenger in the vehicle may have a bias against 'white van man'. Their personal beliefs and a prejudice may influence their statement about how drivers in white vans behave.

From all the data gathered they will produce a reconstruction of the accident. Slowly a picture of the 'reality' of the accident that best fits the evidence gathered is produced.

Using this analogy, I hope you can begin to see that some of those issues I struggled with are not as odd or as wacky as you might first think. The notion, for example, of multiple realities is, when you think about it, logical. We all construct our own realities of life. Large parts intersect with the realities of others, but no two realities will necessarily be the same. As a researcher you may be a witness, or you may only come 'after the event' and examine the data (evidence) but not when the event is happening. The evidence can come in many forms, from measurements to people's recollections. There may have been traffic cameras that recorded the events dispassionately and independently.

As a researcher you are the officer in charge of trying to produce a report that is as independent and unbiased as possible. The aim is to produce a report that relates the 'truth' of any event you investigate.

Structure of this book

This book is spilt into three parts: Part 1 looks at how you access research; Part 2 considers how you analyse research; and Part 3 is about your understanding and appreciation of research.

Part 1: Assessing Research

Chapter 1 sets out a hierarchy of publication types linked to their 'academic worth', for example looking at the differences between an international peer-reviewed journal article and a professional journal and professional magazine article. The purpose of this hierarchy is to begin to form a guide to the reliability of published work, depending on where that work is published.

Chapter 2 describes how to locate good research articles and how to use research databases and collections. It gives advice on formulating good search strings, for example in Google Scholar, and how to refine searches to narrow down the results in order to find more easily recent and relevant articles. There is also important advice on how to avoid plagiarism and academic misconduct, as well as understanding how Harvard referencing, a common system used in the social sciences, works.

Chapter 3 provides advice on how to organise and store articles methodically so that you can more easily retrieve these when compiling literature reviews etc. It sets out different forms of literature review and addresses the important issue of bias. Bias can come in many forms, and identifying bias in research you are reading or controlling for bias in your own research is important. Knowing what forms bias can take helps deal with the problem.

Part 2: Analysing Research

Chapter 4 tackles the difficult issue of differing research paradigms – what they mean and how they can affect research. As noted above, people find terms such as 'ontology', 'epistemology' and 'axiology' confusing and, initially, a bit intimidating. This chapter explains what they mean and then puts them into context by looking at the different research paradigms used in the social sciences. There are too many paradigms to cover concisely in one book, so some of the more common ones – such as post-positivism, interpretivism and pragmatism – are considered.

Chapter 5 deals with different methods and logical argument in research. It does not provide a blow-by-blow account of the various methods that could be used in education research. There are, as stated earlier, many books that explain 'how' to do research and how to implement different methods. This chapter summarises some of the more common methods, but more importantly it looks at logic and reasoning as a way of making sense of the data gathered by the various methods employed in education research. The chapter outlines the 'hourglass' model for research, i.e. the research begins with broad questions that narrow and deepen before finally broadening out again. There is also a comparison between qualitative and quantitative approaches to research.

Chapter 6 is about understanding the language of research and how researchers and academics write. Recognising the various genres of research reporting is critical to understanding the meaning of research. It is often said that academics will use a style of language that is overly complex and utilises polysyllabic, obscure words rather than writing in plain English. There is a degree of truth in this, and one aim of the chapter is to look at why this is done. The chapter will also look at different formats of research article, and then explain the structure of each and how such structures help with maintaining rigour.

Part 3: Appreciating and Understanding Research

Chapter 7 explores a common issue faced by people beginning to engage with research – confusing critical analysis with simply criticising what a researcher has written, or worse still, criticising the researcher as an individual. The purpose of writing a critique or undertaking a critical analysis is to evaluate the work in question. This will, eventually, lead to a greater knowledge and understanding of the topic. Producing a critical analysis requires critical reading and critical writing. Critical analysis is not a description of what the author is saying, but an analysis of the principal argument(s) being presented alongside an assessment of the evidence the researcher uses to support that argument. The chapter looks at common flaws in arguments and describes some of the common logical fallacies that undermine the rigour and integrity of research findings.

Chapter 8 identifies a six-step process for critical analysis and applies this to a published piece of research to provide clear examples of how to read and interpret research. The chapter analyses the article and finishes by describing issues related to secondary sources and relying too heavily on other researchers' interpretations of research.

Finally, Chapter 9 considers the reasons for teaching being regarded as a full profession rather than a job, based on engagement with a specific body of expert knowledge and a theoretical basis for its practices. Research, and understanding how it can influence practice, is part and parcel of professionalism. The chapter continues by looking at ways of researching your own practice as an educator, as well as briefly describing different forms of action research. It ends by looking at the ethics of research that involves children, young adults or vulnerable people.

Each chapter has some further reading and a short bibliography of any research or articles, books, etc., cited within the chapter.

Who would find this book relevant?

The book is intended for final year undergraduate students through to beginning PhD students. It is naturally aimed at Master's-level students and would be beneficial for anyone doing an MA in a social science or humanities field related to children and young people, including trainee teachers on a Post Graduate Certificate in Education (PGCE) or Post Graduate Diploma in Education (PGDipE).

While each chapter of the book is 'self-contained', i.e. there is no specific order in which the chapters *must* be read, it has been organised in a logical way, progressing from the initial finding of the research to considering how to carry out research, while at the same time decoding some of the more obscure terms and concepts that high-quality research generates.

PART 1
ASSESSING RESEARCH

1

The Hierarchy of Research Publications

Chapter aims

- Understand how research is reported
- Look at the variety of publications research may appear within
- Assess the rigour of publications in presenting research/information
- Comprehend what is meant by impact with respect to journals and articles
- Understand the basics of the peer-review system

Introduction

We are bombarded by information to an unprecedented degree. The internet and social media have fundamentally changed how we view information. Research is, at its most basic, information. How research is communicated, which information channels are used and how the message about research evolves or alters each time it is reported will affect how we view research.

Research does not have the privilege of being seen by everyone in its original form. It would be unrealistic to say that all research should be read in its original form. Summaries of research, or the reporting of findings, can be substantially altered according to the mode of communication and who is communicating it. Where original research is published can also impact the level of confidence we should place on the work and its findings. In this chapter, we will examine different levels of publications which form a hierarchy from academic publishing down to popular media such as newspapers and individual blogs online.

Where is research published?

The key question to ask ourselves here is how reliable is the report of the research? This is the point at which we enter the murky, confusing and complex world of academic articles, peer review, impact, professional and everyday writing and publishing.

Before the invention of the internet and the birth of the blog, getting your ideas into print required either an ability to satisfy a publisher that your writing was worth publishing or the ability to self-publish (a process sometimes called 'vanity' publishing). Blogs and websites can be created by anyone and allow almost any opinion to be widely available, with little to no checks, balances or review. The internet provides a platform for a cheap and easy form of vanity publishing.

Broadly, distinguishing between professionally produced online material that is, for want of a better term, 'quality assured' and the writings of a lone 'expert' who may not even have any training in the field that he or she writes about is not difficult. The quality of the writing, spelling, grammar (or lack thereof) and poorly constructed arguments are signs that something has not undergone any form of professional editing process. That said, well-written material could be superficially persuasive, but may not be rigorous or stand up to scrutiny.

Tables 1.1–1.3 list a variety of forms of published output that may contain research or the outcomes of research. Each form has its advantages and disadvantages. For busy professional teachers, directly accessing first-hand research can be time-consuming and potentially difficult as many education research journals are not open access, i.e. the articles are not freely available. The Chartered College of Teaching (CCoT) has made access to first-hand research easier for its members by negotiating their access to a wide variety of education research journals, which should improve the situation for teachers interested in looking at research.

One important yet contentious measure of the value of different forms of publishing is the 'impact factor' that a journal can have. Impact factors are nearly always applied to academic and professional journals (see Box 1.1). We must also differentiate between the 'impact factor' a journal may have and the 'impact' a piece of research may have. The impact that research may have could affect government policy, the practice of teachers or how educational institutions are run. This happens independently from the journal within which research is published.

Table 1.1 Characteristics of academic publications

Academic				
Publication Type	**Main Purpose**	**Content Types**	**Characteristics**	**Review Process**
Journal	• Advancement of knowledge in a field • Report research outcomes	• Reports of research • Case studies • Review articles • Book reviews • Position papers • Theory (new or revised) papers • Methods/ methodology papers • Systematic review • Metastudies	Narrow focus usually restricted to one field or discipline, will contain many citations and a comprehensive bibliography Should contain information on source of funded research or disclosures that may lead to conflicts of interest	Peer reviewed by experts in the field
Handbook/ edited book	• A collection of specific articles to illustrate and guide professionals/ researchers in a field	• Reviews • Research summaries	Very narrow focus on a specialism or specialist area of research Often contains many citations and a bibliography (usually chapter by chapter)	Usually reviewed by the book's editor or specialists in the field
Book chapter(s)	• Easily accessible summary of one topic and there may be one or more chapters on a theme	• Formally written summary on a topic or approach	More general focus either on a subject or discipline, may cover a range of professional aspects, may have some citations or notes	Reviewed by book editor/ publisher

(Continued)

Table 1.1   (Continued)

Academic				
Publication Type	**Main Purpose**	**Content Types**	**Characteristics**	**Review Process**
Conference proceedings	Announcement of new research, disseminating research findings Sharing ideas and research with other practitioners and researchers	• Keynote speeches • Presentations of early/draft papers • Poster display • Round-table discussions • Seminars • Colloquium • Workshops	Usually hosted by an organisation or association with a specific remit Range from small very specialist conferences to large international conferences with specialist groups	Input usually reviewed by a panel of experts after a 'call for papers', and some speakers will be invited to deliver 'keynotes' with no peer review, due to their national/ international standing
Government reports/ research/ publications	Dissemination of findings from reports commissioned by government departments	• Research reports	Research and reports are usually commissioned by a government department with a view to understanding aspects of the subject/discipline and to enable 'evidence-based policy' to be produced Some reports are commissioned to review implemented policy	Internal review may consult with experts Often no formal independent peer-review process

Table 1.2   Characteristics of professional publications

Professional				
Publication Type	**Main Purpose**	**Content Types**	**Characteristics**	**Review Process**
Professional journals	Produced by professional bodies and associations to inform members of new developments and latest news and to disseminate research	• Notes • Review articles • Classroom-based research • Reviews of textbooks or professional books • Some opinion and editorial articles	The journal is often populated by member articles and views and caters directly to the needs of members	Professionals recruited for review to the journal May be academics, researchers or serving professionals

Professional				
Publication Type	**Main Purpose**	**Content Types**	**Characteristics**	**Review Process**
Professional magazines	Produced by professional bodies and associations to inform members of the latest developments, news and policy	• Feature articles • News • Opinion articles • 'Research round-up' of latest ideas • Q&A type articles • Summaries of new policy or legislation	These are more frequently produced items that serve to disseminate important ideas, changes to practice or law within education, and as an outlet for practitioners and others to share opinions on the direction of movement in the field	Minimal review by magazine editor who may or may not call on professional help/ reviews
Professional blogs	Fast online items that can be reactive almost instantly to new positions, directions, policy or research	• Short online items (often 800–1000 words)	Usually written by individuals employed or engaged by the professional body/ associations as a mechanism to air their views on and responses to a very wide variety of subjects They usually adhere to the association/ body view on policy that is agreed by the members or governing members of the association/ body	Minimal review, usually for style, punctuation, grammar
Professional body reports	Longer published items that are specifically commissioned reports to gather, review and disseminate information in order to advance the knowledge and practices within a profession	• Reports will vary in length but generally follow the format for published research	Reports are normally evidenced with a set of citations and a bibliography Reports usually contain information about the methods used and the key research question(s)	Internal review mostly by professional body members

(Continued)

Table 1.2   (Continued)

Professional				
Publication Type	**Main Purpose**	**Content Types**	**Characteristics**	**Review Process**
Theses/ dissertations	Single examinable pieces of work– generally a PhD will be up to 80,000 words and a Master's thesis will vary but is commonly around 15–20,000 words Master's degrees may be taught Master's or research only PhDs are commonly research only, but professional doctorates which include a taught element are becoming more common	• Structured research that includes setting out the research questions, a review of the relevant literature, the methodology and methods used, the data gathered, and analysis of data, discussion and conclusions	A thesis or dissertation is a product of an examination and is written to satisfy the objectives of the exam At Master's-level the expectation is that the student is able to gain an understanding of the research process and identify a research question, and using appropriate methods come to a reasoned and evidenced conclusion There is no expectation that the student will add to the corpus of knowledge about what they are researching at Master's level A PhD is written particularly for three or four people (the supervisor) and two examiners The purpose of the PhD is to add new knowledge or reconceive knowledge, and to satisfy experts in the field of the student's own expertise and ability to carry out research	Supervisor-led reviews during writing then examination A PhD normally requires a viva with an internal examiner and an external expert in the field of study Not peer reviewed for publication

Table 1.3 Characteristics of popular publications

Popular				
Publication Type	**Main Purpose**	**Content Types**	**Characteristics**	**Review Process**
Specialist magazines	To inform a particular sector of society that has a specific interest	• General interest articles • News • Opinion		Editor/sub-editor may or may not have specialist qualifications
General magazines	To inform and entertain targeted sectors in society, sometimes related to age or even gender	• Occasional articles on education – the main intent is usually 'human interest' where the focus is on an individual or group of individuals and their experiences	Usually commissioned pieces written by freelance journalists who may specialise in education but who will also write on a wide variety of other topics	Editor/sub-editor, usually a professional journalist
Newspapers	To inform, entertain and provide up-to-date news and information about what's happening in the world	• Opinion pieces • Reports of policy • News on local/regional/national interest in schools and education generally	Written by a journalist – many have 'education' correspondents who have an interest in education but may not have education qualifications	Editor or section editor, a journalist
Individual blogs	To allow an individual to express an opinion or share knowledge and understanding with a wide audience	• Varying lengths from very short items about a single issue to long rambling pieces that often lack structure or focus • Some individual blogs from practitioners can be very well written and may be useful contributions, but most are not	Often focus on one issue at a time Some are very biased while others strive to be impartial May have citations and a bibliography, but often not The quality of references varies, from self-referencing other blogs or websites that contain unsubstantiated 'evidence' to a good academic standard of referencing	No formal review process Anyone can post a blog about 'anything'

BOX 1.1 IMPACT FACTOR

Many journals advertise their impact factor and use this to attract researchers wishing to publish their research. Impact factors can be calculated in a variety of ways but generally it is a measure of the number of citations articles receive, related to the actual number of articles a journal prints.

The formula for calculating an impact factor is relatively simple:

$$IF_y = \frac{Citations_{y-1} + Citations_{y-2}}{Publications_{y-1} + Publications_{y-2}}$$

IF = Impact Factor; y = year

This formula will work out the average number of citations a published paper receives in a given period - in this case, two years. The higher the number of citations per paper, the higher the impact factor. Journals will also use a five-year period for calculating impact factors, which due to the increased time is more accurate, but impact factors can be distorted by new journals where there is less than two years of data/publishing or where the frequency of publishing is very low, e.g. one journal per year.

The reliability of impact factors is an issue, especially when comparing journals across different disciplines. Some journals have very high citation rates; e.g. in the sciences, the journal *Nature* is very highly regarded and commands many high-quality and ground-breaking articles whose importance leads to high citation rates. In other circumstances, the type of publication can distort the impact factor. For example, review articles are often very highly cited and a journal that publishes many review articles may have a higher impact factor rating as a result. As Amin and Mabe (2000 p.6) state, 'they [impact factors] are not a direct measure of quality and must be used with considerable care'. More recently, Thelwall and Fairclough (2015 p.263) have warned that journal impact factors (JIFs) are 'widely used and promoted but have important limitations. In particular, JIFs can be unduly influenced by individual highly cited articles and hence are inherently unstable'.

A further issue with impact factors concerns journals that are known within the academic world as 'predatory' journals. These try to give the impression that they are *bona fide* academic journals, but exist only to extract money from unwary and inexperienced researchers who are charged high fees for publishing in them. They do not have any credibility, often use fake names and university attributions for their 'editorial boards', and will publish just about anything that is sent to them. They then work hard to extract high fees from the authors. Academics are routinely spammed with emails inviting them to submit an article, even though the journal mentioned has nothing to do with the discipline in which the researcher works. Such 'journals' also routinely promote a fake impact factor to make it seem as if they are a legitimate publishing operation.

Publication types

Academic publications

Academic journals are at the top of any hierarchy for research output. For researchers working in education departments in universities (or any academic discipline) it is often a contractual obligation to produce material for publication in academic journals. Universities in the UK are judged on their academic output via a system called the Research Excellence Framework (REF). This is a huge exercise that judges the output of all lecturers on research contracts and grades this output on a scale from 1* (lowest) to 4* (highest). Not only do journals have a hierarchy, what's published within journals can be rated as well, and articles produced by academics are also rated on the 1*–4* scale. A criticism of this exercise is that it is too cumbersome and that the judgements made may not be reliable. University research funding in the UK is dependent on a good REF outcome, so there is pressure on researchers to publish high-quality research that has wide impact. While this is not the place to debate the pros and cons of the REF, there is no doubt that publication in the academic journals is still seen as the highest quality form of research output.

The structure of a journal article will vary from journal to journal, but generally it will have many if not all of the sections outlined in Box 1.2. Chapter 6 goes into more detail about the writing process for research.

BOX 1.2 A TYPICAL RESEARCH ARTICLE'S STRUCTURE

Abstract

This is a brief summary of the paper and its main findings – usually no more than 200–300 words long.

Introduction

This should set out the problem being addressed and why it is important. There is usually a short statement about what is lacking in our current knowledge and it should state the objectives of the study or the research question(s).

(Continued)

Literature review

Key literature and previous research that is relevant to the study are discussed, critiqued and analysed so that what is currently known about the topic or concept is clearly stated. The literature review will also form the basis for the research questions through the identification of gaps in knowledge or areas where there is disagreement.

Methodology and methods

This section will set out the research paradigm (see Chapter 4) and describe the context and setting of the research. It should then describe the design of the study and the 'population', i.e. who is being studied if it involves people (teachers, children, parents etc.) or what is being studied, e.g. materials such as textbooks or resources etc.

The research should specify what methods were used (see Chapter 5), how any sampling was done, or how the researchers identified the participants within the study.

The next step would be to identify the main study variables and then describe any data collection instruments and procedures. This should be followed by a description of the analysis methods used. In this section the researcher will report on their data collection, how it was done, how much data they have, e.g. whether they used questionnaires, how they recruited people and the response rates they had. There will also be descriptions of the participants (demographic etc.).

Results

This section will present the key findings with respect to the central research question. It may take the form of tables, graphs or a narrative description of the results.

Discussion

This section will restate the main findings of the study and then discuss these with reference to any previous research as outlined in the literature review. The discussion may make reference to the policy and practice implications of the results. There should also be an analysis of the strengths and limitations of the study.

Conclusion

This section should briefly and succinctly set out the main findings, their importance to the field and implications for policy change, along with suggestions for further research or studies.

While many research articles will follow the general research structure as set out in Box 1.2, the structure described is more applicable to a quantitative study rather than a qualitative one. In qualitative studies the results section, rather than being tables of data, and the analysis section, rather than being statistical analysis, may well include a wide range of approaches from discourse analysis to content analysis. While it is tempting to think that quantitative studies will be more rigorous or have outcomes that can be more generally applied, this is not always the case (see Chapter 5). To better understand research published in academic journals, you will need to familiarise yourself with the journal, how it is set out, and how they require articles to be set out. Just as different newspapers have different audiences, preferences and styles, so do academic journals. A good way to understand what a journal requires, and to get a feel for the way it publishes, is to read the 'author guidelines', which each journal will have available on its website. All articles submitted for consideration for publication in academic journals will be peer reviewed.

Peer review

The peer-review process for academic research is considered the best way of ensuring high quality, rigour and expert validation (though this is hotly debated and will be explored briefly later). Articles submitted for publication will be sent for peer review to experts within the field. In most cases a peer review is 'double blind', i.e. the reviewers do not know the name of the author, and the author will not know who is reviewing their submission.

The first stage of peer review is carried out by the journal editor or someone on the editorial board who will initially assess whether the article meets the minimum standards for review, i.e. that it is well written, conforms to the journal requirements for how it has been presented, its word length etc., and that it meets the remit of the journal subjectwise. Having passed this stage, it will be sent out to two (or more) independent reviewers who are experts within the field for consideration. There are normally four responses a reviewer can make:

- Accept for publication with no changes (very rarely happens).
- Accept with minor changes (sometimes used).
- Accept with major changes (often used).
- Reject.

The reviewers are expected to provide a report that would help the author revise the article, improve it, and address any concerns the reviewers may have. The author will then make these adjustments and resubmit the revised article, along with a report on what changes they have made, or if they disagree with a reviewer, a justification for keeping the original point in the article. The process can be a long one, and it is not unusual to have a period of up to a year or more between initial submission and acceptance, and only at that point does the article get scheduled for publication, which can impose further delays. It is possible for research to be at least two years old before it appears in its final published form.

The 'hot debate' over peer review concerns the way the system operates and charges that it can be open to abuse. As noted above, the peer-review system is slow and can be inefficient. Also, reviewers work for the journals unpaid, which means that setting tight deadlines for the return of reviews can be impossible when you are relying on goodwill. My personal experience has seen one article in 'review' for six months before finally being rejected; it then took another year after revisions for it to be finally published in another journal. There are also charges that the reviews produced can be of highly variable quality. As a reviewer, I get asked to read a wide variety of articles and I cannot claim to be an expert in all areas. Where I feel I cannot comment expertly I reject the offer to review, but even where I feel I have some expertise, that does not mean I am expert in all aspects of the field. While reviewers will do their best to be honest and helpful, genuine experts within a field tend to be few in number. In highly specialised fields, this can mean a very small pool of people, which in turn can lead to other issues, e.g. favouritism and jealousy. A reviewer who works out who the author of a paper is may deliberately over-praise or damn a paper. Having more than one reviewer does mitigate this somewhat, but that can also lead to conflicts between reviewers who end up providing contradictory advice.

One move to try and overcome the issues peer review gives rise to is the post-publication review, where an article is initially reviewed for its suitability for publication (well written, grammatical etc.) and there are then calls for an open peer review of the work, with the names of the reviewers known and their comments published with an opportunity for the author to respond. Thus in some cases the review process is not 'blind' in the hope that such transparency will enhance the quality of the reviews.

Other forms of academic publications

There is a range of articles (see Table 1.1) that can be subject to peer review aside from the quantitative and qualitative research articles discussed above. Systematic review articles, for example Linder and Simpson's (2017), summarise research or a concept, comparing and contrasting the positions of researchers. Position papers, such as Hasking et al.'s (2016), are written in order to generate support for an idea – they set out a researcher's basic view of an issue alongside a rationale for that position. A position paper will build a foundation for a researcher's argument. Theoretical papers will set out a new theory (an evidenced explanation) to explain an aspect of children's learning, development or perhaps a pedagogical approach, for example (Sztajn et al., 2012).

Theory papers can also revise established ideas by introducing new evidence. Methodology and methods papers will describe new approaches to research or new ways of gathering and analysing evidence.

A systematic review is a synthesis and appraisal of primary research, for example (Sullivan and Simpson, 2016). The key characteristic of a systematic review is that it uses a clear and specific methodology to both search for and select the articles to be reviewed. The methodology will be designed to minimise bias (see Chapter 3 for a discussion on different forms of bias). Finally, meta-studies or meta-analyses will combine the results of a number of previously published research studies in order to provide a more statistically significant result that could be applied more generally. This is one clear advantage, but a disadvantage is that the methods and methodologies used by the articles in the meta-analysis will vary. A meta-analysis must have a clear set of criteria, a methodology and methods that set out which articles to include and how to handle the data.

Included in the range of academic articles are scholarly handbooks that collect together specific articles as chapters meant to guide researchers and professionals, such as *The SAGE Handbook of Learning* (Scott and Hargreaves, 2015). These are written by academics who are experts in the field and will undergo rigorous peer review. The same is true for book chapters that focus on one theme or issue.

Conference papers, via which new research is often first shared, will undergo some peer review, especially if the papers are collected together and published as conference proceedings. Finally, there are government reports and research findings. These will be specifically commissioned by a government department and address an area of policy that the government is interested in. While these reports are often good research summaries, it is wise to read them with a potential political bias in mind.

Professional publications

There are many professional organisations that teachers can join or serve. These organisations will often publish their own journals and magazines to cover specific issues in which their members are interested. In science education, for example, there is the Association for Science Education (ASE) that produces journals for secondary science teachers (e.g. *School Science Review*) as well as a journal for primary teachers who teach science (*Primary Science Review*). They also produce a specialist magazine, *Education in Science*, with news, views and opinions. Similarly, the Historical Association publishes three professional journals, *Primary History*, *Teaching History* and *The Historian*. They also produce an academic journal, the *International Journal of Historical Learning*. Religious education is served by the professional journal *RE Today*. Nearly all secondary subjects will have associated professional bodies that provide journals and magazines. Contributors to these publications will vary from teachers to university academics as well as freelance consultants and writers. The articles will normally be peer reviewed or at the very least reviewed by the editor of the magazine/journal. The review process is not as rigorous as the academic process, but nevertheless such articles can be very useful. Alongside print journals and magazines, many of these organisations publish blogs. The Chartered College of Teaching publishes *Chartered College Blogs*, featuring articles written by members. This is in addition to its own in-house professional journal, *Impact*.

Professional bodies will occasionally produce reports on specific aspects of their subject. These will be commissioned reports written by members and experts to illuminate a specific idea, concept or issue. While these reports will be reviewed, they will not normally undergo any form of anonymous peer review.

A final category of professional publication is the thesis or dissertation. These are placed within this category as they are principally written to pass an examination at a particular level, either at Master's or doctoral level. They will be rigorous and academic, but it must be remembered that they are written in order to meet a set of examinable criteria. As such, they are not peer reviewed. In the case of a doctorate, there will be an oral examination, the *viva voce* or 'viva', where an expert will explore and challenge the thesis, and the candidate must defend their work.

Popular publications

The most extensive and easiest type of article to find in any search will be a popular article from a magazine, newspaper or online blog. The key purpose of these types of articles is to inform and entertain. Generally, the review process is very simple – it is down to the editor whether or not an article is printed. In the majority of cases they are written by journalists who may or may not have specialist knowledge. Many articles are directly generated from press releases sent out by companies, 'think tanks' or universities, announcing new discoveries, ideas and analysis. By the time something gets into a newspaper, it can be far removed from an original piece of research.

Another issue is that it is usually a press officer's or journalist's take on the research that is the main message reported. This can sometimes come as a surprise to a researcher, with something that was only a minor, insignificant part of their work suddenly becoming a headline and the main message (according to the researcher) being lost. It's worth remembering here that 'boring doesn't sell'. As a researcher, no matter how interesting you think a finding is, if it isn't seen by others as interesting or exciting it will never gain traction in the media. Box 1.3 shows how one piece of research was transformed by the media into something quite different. Research published by think tanks may well have a particular bias depending on who funds the think tank. Not all think tanks will disclose their sources of funding, so determining how 'independent' their work is can be difficult.

BOX 1.3 GENES AND IQ

Publishing research on genes and any link to IQ can be fraught with difficulties when it gets reported in the press. The idea that IQ is linked to genes can be a contentious one. It raises the spectre of racism, and this angle is a popular one for journalists to focus on. Leaving aside the potential for racist attitudes towards IQ and genes, simply putting forward the view that IQ may have a genetic component at all is unacceptable to some people. Research, however, does show a link between IQ and genetics. How such research is reported is crucial to ensuring that the message is not twisted or turned into something that the original research does not claim. Below is one recent story of some research and how various media misreported it, to the extent that the message being given out was not supported by the evidence.

The research

The study (Davies et al., 2018) looked at 300,486 individuals and identified 148 independent genetic loci influencing general cognitive function. They also found 709 individual genes associated with general cognitive function. The team discovered that there was genetic overlap between general cognitive function, reaction time, and many health variables including eyesight, hypertension and longevity.

How the press reported it

The press fixated on one peripheral result: that some genes linked to a higher IQ are also linked to a higher likelihood of poor eyesight.

The Telegraph (Bodkin, 2018) reported a positive correlation of 0.29 (which is, at best, a moderate correlation) as a statement saying that those people who were intelligent were 30% more likely to have genes indicating they required reading glasses, which is not what the report stated. Poor eyesight is not defined as someone requiring reading glasses. The newspaper got the sample size for this study completely wrong, quoting 44,480 when the actual sample size of the study was 300,486. Even simple things went awry, such as the name of one of the lead authors, Gail Davies, being misspelled in two other news reports – becoming Gail Davis in one and Gaye Davies in another.

One online report of the study, by an over-60s health website, had the astonishing headline 'Study Finds Wearing Glasses Actually Makes You Smarter' (Anonymous, 2018). At no point is such a statement made or even implied in the actual research paper; it is an illogical and ridiculous assertion.

(Continued)

The Guardian (Mahdawi, 2018) started reasonably well in describing the research, but suddenly began linking the wearing of glasses to getting off a criminal charge in court. Glasses were used by one barrister who said they 'soften' a person's looks. The article then went on to state there is a lot of empirical evidence that wearing glasses can make a person look more intelligent. There was plenty within the research to fill the required word count for an article, but the link to a barrister to comment on a genetic study may as well have been a link to a barista for all the insight that could be gained.

These may seem like minor errors or issues, but in major research studies, especially where the content can be sensitive, it is important that the correct findings are made clear. Scientists are often so concerned about how their work is interpreted that they decline to engage with the media or go to great lengths to avoid misinterpretation. For example, in another genetic study (Lee et al., 2018), which found 1,271 education-associated genetic variants, the authors produced a long FAQ list to accompany their research (longer than the actual research paper) so that journalists and others reporting on the research could accurately state what the research was saying and, more importantly, what it was not saying. Journalists love an eye-catching headline, so the temptation to say that scientists have found the genes that explain how clever we are is sometimes too tempting. This study did identify hundreds of genetic variants that are associated with math skills and performance on tests of mental abilities, but they are not 'genes for education or intelligence'.

Summary

Not everything that is published is worthwhile, and not everything that is worthwhile is published. Working your way through the maze of research publications can be daunting. Even if you are clear on where to look for the best quality, finding high-quality research in your chosen journal is not guaranteed. In education, there are many who believe that we should approach research in the same way that scientists approach their research. Some believe we should take a 'clinical' approach to research, stating that only randomised controlled trials are worthy of consideration. We will look at this thorny issue later, but needless to say there is no simple answer and no magic bullet in research terms that will deliver simple unambiguous answers to the question of how we should teach or even how children learn.

Education is a complex discipline. People are complex and don't always react and respond in the same way as inanimate objects. In science, it is often possible to make predictions about the outcome of experiments and compare actual outcomes to predictions. People rarely behave in the way you predict or want, making such approaches very difficult. All is not lost however. While education research may not be as conclusive or as easy to generalise from as scientific research, it does not mean we cannot learn from good, well-designed research.

In this chapter we have looked primarily at how research is reported and some of the things you will need to think about with regard to where you will find your research information. Understanding the hierarchy of publications can narrow down the places you need to search and provide a guide for you to access the right material and ignore articles that have little rigour or validity. In the next chapter we will look at how to find appropriate material using well-designed searches and databases.

Further reading

Burke Johnson, R., & Christensen, L. (2016) *Educational Research: Quantitative, Qualitative, and Mixed Approaches* (6th edn) London: Sage (Chapter 4)

This is a detailed textbook on research and how to do research. Chapter 4 looks at sources of research and how to construct literature reviews.

Creswell, J.W., & Creswell, J.D. (2018) *Research Design: Qualitative, Quantitative, and Mixed Methods Approaches* London: Sage (Chapter 2)

Chapter 2 of this book on research methods provides an easy-to-read chapter on choosing and reviewing appropriate literature for your literature review.

Kumar, R. (2014) *Research Methodology: A Step-by-Step Guide for Beginners* London: Sage (Chapter 3)

Chapter 3 in this text looks at the functions of the literature review in research, how to carry out a literature search and how to review the selected literature.

O'Leary, Z. (2014) *Doing Your Research Project* London: Sage (Chapters 3 and 6)

This is a fairly standard textbook on research methods used in undergraduate and postgraduate settings. These two chapters examine how to get started on research and then develop your research questions.

Bibliography

Amin, M., & Mabe, M. (2000) Impact factors: use and abuse *International Journal of Environmental Science and Technology* Vol.1 No.1 pp.1–6

Anonymous (2018) *Study finds wearing glasses actually makes you smarter* [online]. @Startsatsixty. Available at: https://startsat60.com/health/everyday-health/vision/wearing-glasses-make-you-smarter-university-of-edinburgh-study (accessed 12th February 2020)

Bodkin, H. (2018) 'Glasses Wearers Really Are More Intelligent – It's in the Genes', *The Telegraph* May 30th

Davies, G., Lam, M., Harris, S.E., et al. (2018) Study of 300,486 individuals identifies 148 independent genetic loci influencing general cognitive function *Nature Communications* Vol.9 No.1 p. 2098

Hasking, P.A., Heath, N.L., Kaess, M., et al. (2016) Position paper for guiding response to non-suicidal self-injury in schools *School Psychology International* Vol.37 No.6 pp. 644–663

Lee, J.J., Wedow, R., Okbay, A., Kong, E., Maghzian, O., Zacher, M., Nguyen-Viet, T.A., Bowers, P., Sidorenko, J., Linnér, R.K. and Fontana, M.A. (2018) Gene discovery and polygenic prediction from a genome-wide association study of educational attainment in 1.1 million individuals *Nature Genetics* Vol.50 No.8 pp.1112–1121

Mahdawi, A. (2018) 'Wearing Glasses May Really Mean You're Smarter, Major Study Finds', *The Guardian* May 30th

Scott, D. & Hargreaves, E. (2015) *The SAGE Handbook of Learning* Los Angeles, CA: Sage

Sullivan, A.L., & Simonson, G.R. (2016) A systematic review of school-based social-emotional interventions for refugee and war-traumatized youth *Review of Educational Research* Vol.86 No.2 pp.503–530

Sztajn, P., Confrey, J., Wilson, P.H., & Edgington, C. (2012) Learning trajectory based instruction: toward a theory of teaching *Educational Researcher* Vol.41 No.5 pp.147–156

Thelwall, M., & Fairclough, R. (2015) Geometric journal impact factors correcting for individual highly cited articles *Journal of Informetrics* Vol.9 No.2 pp.263–272

2
Where To Find Good Research and How To Reference It Properly

Chapter aims

- Describe how to formulate good search strings
- Gain awareness of different databases of education research
- Understand the benefits of using a bibliographic database
- Know the difference between a bibliography and a reference list
- Learn how to avoid plagiarism and academic misconduct
- Understand how the Harvard referencing system works

Introduction

Finding good research that meets your needs is not a simple task. The volume of research being published is immense. Understanding how to search for relevant research and having a way of determining quality are necessary skills that help you avoid wasting time or reading irrelevant literature. Having determined a hierarchy of publications, we are beginning to work out one aspect of quality – how rigorously the work has been reviewed prior to publication. In this chapter we will look at how to find good research, organise it so that it can be retrieved at ease, and then properly reference this when you report on what you have found.

If you have written any type of academic essay, whether it's for a degree or a higher degree, you will understand that accessing good research that is relevant to the topic you are studying is essential. A common mistake made by undergraduate (and many postgraduate) students is including out-of-date or irrelevant research. In this chapter we will look at how to search for relevant material, at strategies for searches that provide the most relevant literature, and list some of the databases and search engines that will allow you to access research articles. We will then move on to consider how to keep track of the articles you find in order to build up a database of references that can be used to compile a bibliography or reference list.

How will I know what to search for?

The simple answer to this question is that only you can really know what it is you are looking for. If you are embarking on a search for information about a topic, concept or idea it is best to formulate your initial search as a question (or series of questions). Even a simple question will generate a number of keywords that will form the basis of your search. As an example, the box below outlines the process of generating search terms from a simple question about primary teachers' confidence in teaching science.

BOX 2.1 FINDING GOOD RESEARCH

To illustrate a search process for finding good research on a particular issue, we'll use the following question:

What do we know about primary teachers' confidence in teaching science at Key Stage 2?

From this question we can generate keywords to use in an online search.

Keywords: primary; teacher; science; Key Stage 2; confidence; teaching; learning

There are probably many more keywords that could be used to interrogate databases for research, but we will keep the list relatively short for the purposes of this explainer.

The fact that we are thinking about Key Stage 2 makes this a topic relevant to the UK rather than internationally. However, it would be a mistake to rule out research from other countries at this stage. Insights and research from other countries can help inform us about what we may see or find in the UK. It is also worth noting that the term 'primary' may have a specific meaning for teachers in the UK, but overseas the term 'elementary' may be more commonly used.

Having sorted out your initial question, it's a good idea to spend time thinking about as many keywords as you can that may be relevant. How you do this will be a matter of preference – some people like to use mind maps, others simply produce lists.

If you are registered as a student and have access to a university library, this would be the best starting place for your search for good research. If you have no affiliations or professional memberships to access journals, then Google Scholar is the best starting point. You can also link a Google Scholar profile (see Figure 2.1) to your university library to make accessing journals your university subscribes to easier.

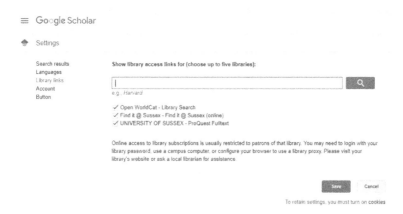

Figure 2.1   Google Scholar settings to link to your institution library

(Google and the Google logo are registered trademarks of Google LLC, used with permission)

Why Google Scholar?

Using keywords, a simple search can be formulated by putting these directly into a search engine. The problem is that a general Google search using just some of the keywords above will generate over 30 million hits. It is also not specific to articles or books. It will cover anything and everything that could be put on the internet, including videos, sound files and images. To better target research that will be useful, you will need a more specific search engine and some basic rules for generating good search terms. This is where Google Scholar comes into its own: as its description states, 'it searches articles, theses, books, abstracts from academic publishers, professional societies, online repositories, universities and other web sites' (Anonymous, 2018). It also pre-screens a lot of irrelevant material out, leaving you to concentrate on finding the best articles to suit your needs.

Basic search rules

There are a number of conventions to be aware of when using a search engine. The following conventions and rules apply to Google Scholar and Google but will be relevant to other search engines as well:

1. Choose as wide a range of descriptive words as you can. Too few words will give poor results. Select nouns to avoid 'stop words' (these are words that most search engines ignore, such as 'is', 'isn't', 'him', 'her', 'and', 'an', 'any', etc., as they slow down searches). Be specific, especially if you are using professional terms.
2. Searches are not case sensitive. Keywords may be entered in lower or upper case or a combination of both, e.g. Mathematics, MATHEMATICS. One exception to this is the Boolean operator OR which can be used to include one or more terms in a search; e.g. with primary OR elementary the OR must be in caps. (NB: A Boolean search uses terms such as AND, OR, NOT, BETWEEN and WITHIN. These are called 'operators' and they specify what words the results of your search should or should not contain, and how close your search terms should be to each other. The term comes from the name of the man who invented the form of logic used, George Boole (1815–1864).)
3. When you enter a list of words the Boolean operator AND is assumed; e.g. primary AND teachers AND science is the same as primary teachers science when entered in a search box.
4. The order in which you insert your search terms matters. Google ranks the search terms in order, i.e. the first word ranks higher than the second, the second ranks higher than the third, etc., so primary science will return slightly different results than science primary. Google ignores most punctuation and symbols, but there are exceptions: the use of a hyphen or underscore such as *sister-in-law* or *end_of_file* and programming language symbols or musical terms (C#).

5. Google uses automatic word stemming.
6. Google does not allow wildcards to be used for variable ends of words, but it does search for all possible word variations.
7. Wildcards can be used in searches to substitute for whole words, e.g. *Alfred * Wallace* would return the following:
   a. Alfred Wallace
   b. Alfred Russel Wallace
   c. Alfred R Wallace
8. Use double quotation marks to search for precise phrases in the order in which you input them, e.g. "primary teachers' confidence" or "key stage 2 science".
9. Use a minus sign to exclude words, e.g. primary - elementary (note there is no space between the minus sign and the word to be excluded).

Table 2.1 provides a more complete list of the various search operators you can use to narrow down your search.

Table 2.1 Google* search engine operators

Operator (where present, colons should be used and search terms should have no space after the colon)	What it does	How it changes your search parameters
allinurl:	Restricts your search to the terms being found in the URL only	This is a very specific search that will only return webpages that contain your search terms in the web address or URL (Universal Resource Locator)
inurl:	Searches for your terms in the URL and on the page	This widens the search to include the search terms on the page as well as in the web address
allintitle:	Restricts the search to the terms being found only in a title on the webpage or document	This is useful if you know one or more words in the title of an article you want to retrieve but may not know the exact title
intitle:	This restricts the search to all the keywords being present in the title of the article or webpage	This search allows you to be less precise about words in the title
allintext:	This restricts the search to all the keywords being present in the text of the article or webpage	This is used when you want the text to include all of the specified search words
intext:	This widens the search to keywords being present in the text	This is used when you want to ensure one or more words are used in the text of an article or on a page

(Continued)

Table 2.1   (Continued)

Operator (where present, colons should be used and search terms should have no space after the colon)	What it does	How it changes your search parameters
filetype:	Allows you to search for particular filetypes by specifying the filetype extension, e.g. docx pdf pptx xlsx (older documents may have the extension doc, xls or ppt)	This will allow you to narrow your search to files that you can download easily – it is useful for searching for copies of research papers placed on university websites by authors
site:	This narrows the results to a particular site	This allows your search to be restricted to a particular site, e.g. a university website: primary science teacher confidence site:sussex.ac.uk or a domain: primary science teacher confidence site:ac.uk
Define:	Provides a definition of a specified word	This is a quick way to access a dictionary definition – it will also provide searches of online dictionaries, so you can use your preferred dictionary
Author:	Specify a particular author to search for	This option allows you to find anything written by a specific author – use whole names rather than just a surname
Double quotation marks " "	Search for a precise phrase	Only articles or pages with the precise phrase contained within the double quotes will be returned
Minus sign (–)	Excludes the word immediately after the minus sign	This is helpful to exclude articles that are irrelevant, but which may contain other search terms that you want to include, for example Primary science –mathematics will return only results that contain primary science – if the article or page has the word 'mathematics', it will be excluded from the results
OR	Alternatives	This allows you to search for a range of words or alternatives, for example (Primary OR elementary OR key stage 2) science This returns results for science articles that have one or more of the search terms in brackets – brackets can be used to group search operators

Operator (where present, colons should be used and search terms should have no space after the colon)	What it does	How it changes your search parameters
Numrange (..)	Search for a range of numbers	This is useful to specify a date range, e.g. 2010..2012
Asterisk (*)	Stands for a word or a few words	This is a wildcard that can be used to return a search with some unknown words, e.g. Alfred * Wallace would return pages that list the following combinations of names: Alfred Wallace Alfred R Wallace Alfred Russel Wallace
AROUND (n)	Proximity search	This is an advanced search operator that allows you to look for terms that feature near to another term, e.g. primary AROUND (5) science would return results where the word 'primary' is found within 5 words of the term 'science' – you can vary the proximity by increasing or decreasing the number (n)

(*Google and the Google logo are registered trademarks of Google LLC, used with permission)

Once you have your basic research question(s) and you have generated some key-words there are several ways you can gain access to research. Open Access research is becoming more common. This means that there are no restrictions on who can access and download copies of the research articles. A lot of research, however, is still found behind 'paywalls'. If you are affiliated with a university, then generally you can access the journals to which the university subscribes for free. The Chartered College of Teaching, as noted in Chapter 1, has also come to an arrangement with many jour-nals for free access for its members. It is possible to buy a copy of the research article from a journal, but this can be expensive. Some journals will also allow access for a short period of time for a small fee. Often, a pre-published copy of the article can be found by visiting the website of the academic who wrote the research. It is also not uncommon for academics to receive requests for a copy of their article by e-mail; many will oblige, but you may have to wait for a reply.

Developing good searching habits and using search operators is essential for cutting down on time wasted trawling through irrelevant search results on the internet. It also helps to keep you focused on what you should be looking for rather than going off at a tangent when you spot something that may be 'interesting' but is not relevant.

Google Scholar

Google Scholar allows you to search for academic and scholarly material, including books, journal articles, conference papers and proceedings, book chapters and theses, on a wide range of subjects. The results are sorted by relevance based on several variables, including full-text matching, place of publication, author(s), and how often the article has been cited by other authors.

There are several advantages to using Google Scholar over a straightforward Google search:

1. It excludes millions of websites and blogs which, as discussed in Chapter 1, are not necessarily the best source of research or scholarly material.
2. It will allow you to directly access open access papers to download (usually as pdf documents).
3. It can be linked to a university library (see Figure 2.1) to allow you to access journals for which your university has subscriptions. Google Scholar will also allow you to add search results to your own online library to access at a later date.
4. You can download citation files that can be added to bibliographic databases (see below) or you can copy and paste some already formatted citations directly into a bibliography or reference list.

Google Scholar also has an advanced search option which is another way of narrowing your search parameters (see Figure 2.2). However even this will still return a large

Figure 2.2   Google Scholar advanced search

(Google and the Google logo are registered trademarks of Google LLC, used with permission)

number of potential articles (see Figure 2.3), so it is worth understanding the anatomy of the Google Scholar page (see Figure 2.4) in order to easily identify ways of locating, saving and accessing research.

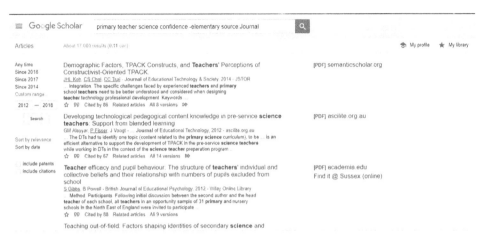

Figure 2.3   Search returns using the advanced search from Figure 2.2

(*Google and the Google logo are registered trademarks of Google LLC, used with permission)

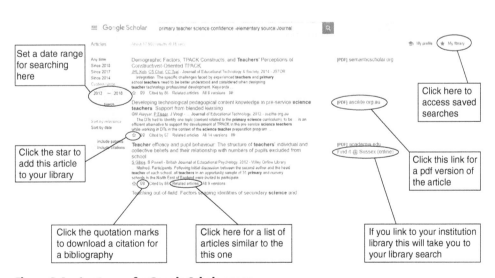

Figure 2.4   Anatomy of a Google Scholar page

(Google and the Google logo are registered trademarks of Google LLC, used with permission)

Locating research using online databases

While Google and Google Scholar will deliver a wide range of research, there are a number of other databases and search engines that specialise in locating scholarly and academic work. Table 2.2 lists some of the databases and sources of materials (articles, video streaming services) that relate to education. This is not a comprehensive and complete list, but it does set out some of the more common and widely accessible databases.

Table 2.2   Selected education-related databases (source: University of Sussex Library guide for education)

Education related database name	Description
ASSIA (Applied Social Sciences Index and Abstracts)	An indexing and abstracting tool covering health, social services, psychology, sociology, economics, politics, race relations and education. Updated monthly, a comprehensive source of social science and health information for the practical and academic professional.
British Education Index (BEI)	Provides information on research, policy and practice in education and training in the UK.
Digital Theatre Plus	Offers streamed films of leading British theatre productions for educational use in schools, colleges and universities. Each production is supported by additional content, including interviews with the creative and production teams and written study guides.
Education Endowment Foundation	Summaries of education evidence, offering teachers 'best bets' of what has worked most effectively to boost the attainment of disadvantaged pupils.
Education-line	A collection of free full text documents which are relevant to the study, practice and administration of education at a professional level.
Educational Resources Information Center (ERIC)	Provides extensive access to educational-related literature. The ERIC database corresponds to two printed journals: *Resources in Education* (RIE) and *Current Index to Journals in Education* (CIJE).
JSTOR	Contains a trusted archive of important scholarly journals, primarily in the humanities and social sciences.
Project Muse	Access to high-quality humanities, arts, and social sciences journals from scholarly publishers.
SAGE Journals online	Search function for all SAGE journal articles.
SAGE Research Methods online	A research methods tool created to help researchers, faculty and students with their research projects.
Scopus	Abstracts and citations for over 22,000 peer-reviewed titles from more than 5,000 international publishers in the scientific, technical, medical, and social sciences.
Web of Science	Access to the Science Citation Index, Social Sciences Citation Index and Arts & Humanities Citation Index.

The same rules for searching databases apply as for searching Google Scholar. Keywords are crucial and the operators will also be useful to narrow down your search parameters.

When you use various search engines, if you are logged on using either an institution account or, for Google, a Google account, many databases and search engines will allow you to save your searches. If you are accessing literature over a period of time, it is easy to forget which keywords and combinations of terms you have used to conduct searches. Keeping a record of your searches is a good move as this prevents you from duplicating work and wasting time repeating searches.

Whichever method you use to source research material, you are likely to have many more articles and search results than you can easily manage. At this point you will need to use further criteria to narrow your search. If your search engine or database allows you to gather together relevant literature into an online 'library', make use of this to have an easily accessible list of articles. Chapter 7 will provide advice on how your articles can be initially sifted and then considered in more depth using critical analysis. At this stage, good record keeping is essential.

Record keeping and citations

At noted above, keeping a record of your searches and the articles, books or chapters you want to read is simply good housekeeping. Another habit to get into when accessing research is making sure you keep a bibliographic record of all your research so that, at a later point, when you use material from it in an essay or report, you can provide a proper citation. This is particularly important when writing assignments, essays or your own research articles so that you avoid any possible charges of plagiarism.

There are many ways of creating a database of references for use in citations. They range from using commercial programs to free open source software, or just keeping a list in a word document or spreadsheet (the latter two methods are not advised for maintaining large numbers of records). Commercial programs such as Endnote can be costly for individuals, but free if you are affiliated to an institution that subscribes; but alternatives such as as RefMan, RefWorks, Mendeley or Zotero are also available, some for free. For users of Microsoft Word (MS Word), there is an inbuilt bibliography database that you can populate and use. To access this, go to the 'references' tab. The options 'Manage Sources' and 'Style' will allow you to enter details of the reference and choose which reference style to use.

The benefits of using a reference management system are clear. It keeps a record of what you have consulted and read. In many systems, you can also add notes about what you have covered. Some of the more sophisticated ones, such as Endnote, also allow you to attach a pdf or Word copy of the article to the reference entry.

The databases will also allow you to insert a reference within your own essay, assignment or thesis using a free plug-in program for word processors like MS Word. From this you can create a properly formatted bibliography or reference list. If you are writing an article for publication in a journal, different journals may have different requirements for their bibliography/reference lists. A reference management database allows you to reformat a list easily and quickly to conform to a journal's 'house style'.

Using a database to store and format your references saves a lot of hard work and can cut down on mistakes when compiling bibliographies and reference lists. This leads to an obvious question – what's the difference between a bibliography and a reference list?

Bibliographies and reference lists

If you compare a bibliography and a reference list, the difference between them may not be apparent. Both list articles, books, reports, websites etc., usually in alphabetical order, using authors' surnames, or in number order according to the order in which they appear within the text of the article. The crucial difference is that a bibliography contains all the works cited in an article or essay, and may contain other works consulted but not specifically quoted or cited in an essay. A reference list contains only those works actually cited in the article or essay, and no other works that may have been used for background reading.

Different publishers have different ways in which they would like works to be cited. One of the most commonly used systems is the Harvard reference system that uses an '(author-date)' system of in-text referencing, also called 'parenthetical referencing'. The resulting bibliography or reference list uses authors' surnames in alphabetical order. Contrary to popular belief it is not called Harvard after the US university. There is no connection between the two. The system is reputed to have been invented by the zoologist Edward Laurens Mark (1847–1946), who would have used the library at Harvard's Museum of Comparative Zoology (Chernin, 1988). The books and articles in the library were catalogued using an 'author-date' system. In an article on slugs in 1881, Mark used the '(author-date)' system for the first time. It is assumed, though not proven, that Mark copied the library system as a handy way of referencing the works he consulted when writing his own article.

The Harvard system is widely used across the sciences and social sciences and in many humanities. Other popular systems include MLA (Modern Languages Association), APA (American Psychological Association), Chicago, Vancouver, and the numerical style. A number of good books on academic writing skills will cover the basics of good referencing and citations, such as Osmond (2016) and Pears (2016). In this book, the Harvard system is used.

Creating a reference database

When you read an interesting book or article, there are some basic steps you can take to make sure you keep at least the basic information necessary for referencing and citations.

The three key pieces of information you need are the name of the author, the title of the book or article and the publisher. For reference database software, like Endnote or Mendeley, much more information can be collected to make your citations and references as accurate as possible. For books, the edition, the place of publication, and sometimes the imprint, provide useful data. A location is used for referencing as editions published in different countries may differ, e.g. a book first published in the UK and then subsequently published in the USA may have been edited and changes made to suit a different audience.

BOX 2.2 USING BIBLIOGRAPHIC DATABASES

Endnote, a reference or bibliographic database, allows you to store a wide range of different types of publications, from webpages to books, book chapters, journal articles and government documents. It's worth noting that the system requires more information than you would normally use within a reference list. This is because the system has hundreds of templates for different types of publications, and different journals require different bits of information in their references.

In essence, the more information you can store, the better. If you are storing information about online sources, articles or webpages, it is important to put the latest date on which you accessed the material. Webpages, blogs etc. are regularly archived or even deleted. While it is possible to view deleted pages through systems such as the 'wayback machine', using an access date allows the reader to know when the page was last freely available. If your chosen reference management system has a function that allows you to store a pdf or word copy of the article, it makes sense to do this when you collect the citation data.

How you organise your reading will very much depend on how you prefer to work. Whether you organise in themes, chapters, concepts, authors or chronologically is for you to decide. Chapter 3 will help you develop a methodology for your research reading. How you read and analyse research is a skill that can be learned, and with practice this will improve your ability to spot defects and flaws in published work as well as recognise well-constructed and designed research studies (see also Chapters 7 and 8).

Avoiding academic misconduct with good citation practices

Correctly citing your work is essential if you wish to avoid charges of plagiarism. Plagiarism is using the work or ideas of someone else without credit. Being systematic about how you cite the work of others is essential. It is good academic practice and avoids possible charges of academic misconduct, if you are on a degree or award-bearing course, or simply breaching copyright if you are writing online.

Universities will have guidance on how to properly cite the articles, books etc., and you should follow their guidance where possible. What is set out below is general guidance for citation.

How to reference

Good referencing and citation show academic integrity and will provide an indication of the hard work you put into understanding research. All of us are at some point influenced by the ideas and thinking of others. Good referencing just acknowledges this and sets apart your original ideas and opinions from the ideas and opinions of others.

Generally, when writing a report or assignment people will summarise or paraphrase the work they have read. This still requires a reference to the original work. Where direct quotations are used this must be made clear, and where possible any reference or citation must also include a page number. In effect, what you are doing in referencing and citing the work of others is substantiating any knowledge or theoretical positions you are using in your own writing. It also shows the breadth of reading you have undertaken. One of the most common ways of referencing, as noted above, is the '(author-date)' system of in-text referencing. Box 2.3 shows how referencing and citation works in practice.

BOX 2.3 IN-TEXT, HARVARD STYLE REFERENCING

The following excerpts show how in-text referencing works in practice. The first example acknowledges that a brief summary of an idea comes from another author.

Example 1:

> The nature of science is a difficult concept and one that promotes debate and disagreement among scientists, philosophers and historians of science (Williams, 2011).

The second example shows how an author can be cited as part of the narrative.

Example 2:

> Should we 'believe' in evolution, or just accept it? This is the basic premise Williams (2015) puts forward in a paper examining the nature of acceptance and belief, from a philosophical perspective.

The third example cites a webpage (blog) rather than a published article.

Example 3:

> The Grammar school debate has just been re-ignited with the recent decision of Nicky Morgan, Secretary of State for Education, to allow an 'annexe' to be built for the Weald of Kent Grammar school. Whilst many argue that this is about social mobility, in an online blog, Williams (2015a) argues that it's more about social stability than mobility.

The final example shows how a direct quotation should be referenced.

Example 4:
Many evangelical Christians ask why scientists believe in evolution. In an article on belief versus acceptance, it was postulated that science is about the acceptance of evidence, rather than a belief system:

> It would be preferable to accept evolution, rather than believe because of the weight of scientific evidence in its favour. Gravity is accepted because of everyday experiences of it; people drop things and they always fall downwards. People also accept the existence of atoms even though they are unable to see them in any detail. (Williams, 2015 p.329)

Notice that the dates of some of the items referenced in the above examples are from the same year, 2015, and in Example 3 the date is followed by the letter 'a' to differentiate it from the previous entry with the same date.
The three articles would appear in a reference list or bibliography as follows:

Example 5:

Williams, J.D. (2011) *How Science Works: Teaching and Learning in the Science Classroom* London: Bloomsbury

(Continued)

Williams, J.D. (2015a) Evolution versus creationism: a matter of acceptance versus belief *Journal of Biological Education* Vol.39 No.3 pp.322–333

Williams, J.D. (2015b) The Grammar School Debate is not about mobility, but stability *James's Thinking Space: living in a Darwinian paradigm* URL: https://jamesdwilliams.wordpress.com/2015/10/18/the-grammar-school-debate-is-not-about-mobility-but-stability/ (accessed August 20th 2018)

The bibliography or reference list is ordered alphabetically, by author surname. Note that it is a mixture of italics and non-italics. This is a source of confusion for many people – which bit is *italicised* and why? The short answer is what you take off the shelf in a library if the item was printed is italicised. For a book, it's the name of the book; for a journal article, it's the name of the journal. For websites, as noted above, the date you last accessed the website, before you complete the assignment or report, is given.

Summary

There is a lot of good research available, but it is a case of not seeing the trees due to the forest. Much of what is written online can be a distraction, and looking for research online does not always quickly or easily deliver good, high-quality research. Knowing which are the reliable and useful databases, and then discovering how to effectively and efficiently search these to screen out the unnecessary articles, is a matter of practice and experience. Over time, you will get to know and understand the various journals and what they deliver, as well as developing a feeling for the level of intellectual rigour of the articles they publish.

It is worth experimenting with the various search operators to understand how they can be used to narrow down the field of available articles. The better your keywords are, the better the information you will retrieve from the databases. A widely used and freely available search engine, Google Scholar is one of the best ways to start a search.

Keeping abreast of research also means keeping a database of what you have read. The more organised you are about this, the easier it is to retrieve the information you want quickly. The better your record keeping, the less likely you are to be accused of misconduct. One problem many people encounter is 'cut and paste misconduct' – you cut and paste a useful quotation or passage into a file but forget to note where it comes from. Eventually, you may even forget that it was a cut and paste to begin with. If you then incorporate this into your work without proper attribution it is plagiarism – regardless of your intent, you are still guilty of misconduct.

How you reference articles, books etc. is down to the institution you are producing an assignment for. They will normally specify the system to use. In this chapter and throughout this book, the Harvard system is used as it is a widely adopted system.

Further reading

Osmond, A. (2016) *Academic Writing and Grammar for Students* London: Sage

This useful guide shows you how to improve the quality of your work at university fast by identifying and using the correct use of English grammar and punctuation in your academic writing.

Pears, R. (2016) *Cite Them Right: The Essential Referencing Guide* (10th revised and expanded edn) London: Palgrave

This is a comprehensive, easy-to-use guide to referencing. It promotes the skills of identifying and referencing information sources and avoiding plagiarism.

Bibliography

Anonymous (2018) About Google Scholar [online] Google Scholar. Available at: https://scholar.google.com/intl/en/scholar/about.html (accessed August 20th 2018)

Chernin, E. (1988) The "Harvard system": a mystery dispelled *British Medical Journal* Vol.297 No.6655 p.1062

Osmond, A. (2016) *Academic Writing and Grammar for Students* London: Sage

Pears, R. (2016) *Cite Them Right: The Essential Referencing Guide* (10th revised and expanded edn) London: Palgrave

3

Organising Your Research Reading and Avoiding Bias

Chapter aims

- Understand different forms of literature review
- Explore what is meant by bias in research
- Examine different categories of bias

Introduction

It is one thing collecting research, but it's quite another organising it so that you can manage the reading in a way that is meaningful. In this chapter we will look at how you can devise a methodology for your reading that will help you review the literature you have gathered. One of the main things to be aware of is bias. Bias is a natural state in people – we all have bias. Knowing and understanding what bias is and how to recognise different forms of bias is one way of ensuring that when you read material, you do not simply reject it because it goes against your natural bias. Even scientists, who would claim neutrality and work hard to eliminate bias, still have to be mindful of their own bias and take steps to minimise it in their day-to-day work.

Devising a methodology for reviewing your literature

In gathering research literature, you will have a purpose. In Chapter 2 this was related to a research question or questions. In reviewing literature, you need to have in mind what sort of outcome you want. You will need to review your research systematically and for this you will require a methodology. That methodology will be linked to the outcome intended from reading your literature. There are several types of literature reviews that you could produce, each with a specific purpose. That purpose will then guide your reading and how you review the articles you find.

BOX 3.1 TYPES OF LITERATURE REVIEW

A good literature review provides an overview of a subject, concept or idea. It should also show how your own ideas fit with the views and ideas of the authors you have drawn upon. Literature reviews can be written in several different ways, each with a specific purpose in mind. The following categories of review are adapted from descriptions provided by the University of California (Labaree, 2018).

Argumentative review

This type of review specifically seeks out arguments that refute a known position or contradict an established view or theory. It is not a balanced view, i.e. it won't take in contra arguments but is specifically designed to undermine a position, so

---

that the writer can then use this to support an opposing view, perhaps something they have developed. A major issue with this type of review is bias. Necessarily, this type of review ignores work that is not supportive of the new view and focuses on undermining an established view.

Historical review

This form of review seeks to trace the establishment and development of ideas over time. It looks at an issue or concept and tries to deliver a balanced view of how the ideas have changed over time. The point of such a review is to place ideas in their context, both in time and place.

Integrative review

This type of review brings together what is known about an idea, concept, theory etc. It is written from several perspectives so that a new or original synthesis of the ideas being discussed is made.

Methodological review

This is an analytical form of review that does not simply summarise or paraphrase what the findings of any research were, but analyses the content so that we can discover how they came to the findings, what the logic of their conclusions is, and whether the evidence supports the conclusions.

Systematic review

This simply provides an overview of the knowledge and understanding that currently exists about a particular idea, concept, phenomenon etc. One of the key elements of this type of review is a critique of the methods used in other research to see whether these are compatible and whether, as a result, the outcomes from other research can be combined to provide a more reliable picture.

Theoretical review

This type of review will look at any and all theory that has been developed to explain an issue, concept, theory, phenomenon etc. It seeks to uncover whether there is any relationship between different theoretical approaches, and it can be used to develop new hypotheses (testable ideas) from existing theory in an effort to advance our knowledge and understanding. This type of review can be useful to point out where theory is absent or where theories may overlap. It may also be the basis for a view that existing theory is inadequate in explaining our current understanding.

If you are not writing a literature review for a specific purpose (an assignment or essay) it is still a good idea to organise your literature in a logical way, perhaps as a theme or to support the chapter of a thesis or organised by concept, idea or theory. During the collection and reading of any research, you must be aware of bias – if not of any possible bias in the research, certainly of your own bias.

Bias in qualitative research

Bias can affect the validity and rigour of any research. In quantitative research its design is normally predicated on these two characteristics being 'built in'. Features such as 'randomisation' or having 'controls' are designed to increase validity and rigour. In reviewing quantitative research such features can be identified. Quantitative research will contain statistical tests which, if you understand the basics of statistics, will also provide indications of the validity and rigour of the research as well as confidence in the findings.

Qualitative research can suffer from what appears to be a 'crisis of authority' (Lather, 1993 p.683). Qualitative research can be characterised as invalid if it does not conform to what is seen as a norm for quantitative research. Norris (1997 p.173) suggests that when we consider validity in relation to qualitative research we should 'focus on error and bias'. A common criticism of research design in qualitative studies is that sampling does not always reflect the diversity of the population being studied, and because of this generalisations cannot be made, no matter how good the findings. This is especially so if the research is in the form of a case study.

Case study research

A case study is not a method in itself. It requires the use of various methods to allow a researcher to look at 'something' – the case – in depth. Case study research is, by its nature, an intensive approach to research that seeks depth rather than breadth, and generalisability is not one of the key outcomes.

Stake (1995) distinguishes between three main types of case study, i.e. intrinsic, instrumental and collective. His idea is not to categorise case studies as such, but to point to the fact that the methods used to complete the case study will differ. 'Intrinsic' case studies, in Stake's terms, are done from the researcher's intrinsic interest in the subject, or case, under study. 'Instrumental' case studies are carried out to gain insight, and 'collective' refers to several case studies designed to form an overall understanding of something. This contrasts with Thomas (2016 pp.12–14), who describes the properties of a case study in three ways, as a 'container', 'situation' or 'event', and then ultimately as an 'argument'. We will look at case studies in more depth in Chapter 6.

BOX 3.2 HOW GOOD ARE POLITICAL POLLS?

We all know that political polls are not the most reliable predictors of election outcomes. Such polls use well-defined samples that are supposedly representative of the voting population as a whole. A lot of time and effort, according to those who conduct polls, goes into trying to ensure that samples are representative, that bias is eliminated, and that the methods used do not inadvertently include or exclude certain groups. The main question people have with regard to polls is how, if you are only sampling a small number of the whole population (e.g. 1,000 or 2,000 people for a general election when millions of people can vote), can you possibly have reliability, validity and rigour? One answer is that you don't have to drink a whole vat of wine to know whether it's good or bad. A small sample will do, provided the sample is gathered properly. We know, however, that polling is not reliable. We tend to aggregate a number of polls in the hope that the aggregate will be a better indicator. Even this does not necessarily result in an accurate prediction of outcomes. Should any poll actually make a reasonably accurate prediction, our tendency is to reject this as a coincidence or a fluke. On the one hand, we are naturally sceptical of polls (a form of quantitative 'research' that uses statistical methods) but on the other, we are also critical of research that does not follow the norms of quantitative ways of ensuring reliability, validity and rigour. The common factor is that we are dealing with people, and with what those people are thinking, how they view things such as life, politics etc. People will often not behave in predictable ways. We cannot rely 100% on what they may say to us in response to our questions. When exit polls are taken, for example, people may or may not tell the truth about which candidate they voted for or the party they support. And in polls, even if people are telling us what they believe to be true or correct, how do we know that their views have not been biased in some way?

What is bias?

A simple definition of bias is giving undue weight or consideration in favour of or against a single thing, person or group when compared to another. The result of that bias will then be an unfair outcome. There are a number of different forms of bias (see below). You will need to be aware of these when evaluating research and to understand that bias, while common, is different from prejudice.

Prejudice is an unreasonable and detrimental opinion based neither on reason nor on evidence. Prejudice is often characterised by a prejudgement or opinion formed before becoming aware of any facts or evidence. Examples of prejudice would be things like racism, sexism, classism etc. We would hope and expect that no respectable publisher, research body or professional organisation would ever publish prejudicial research. It could be the case, however, that prejudiced research on less reputable blogs and websites may well end up in your search results, so this is something to bear in mind.

We will all display bias at some time. We may favour Sky News over BBC, ITV or Channel 4 News. Some of this might have to do with the individuals presenting the news, but it could also be based on how the story is interpreted or how one broadcaster appears to favour (or not) one view over another. Ideally our news should be neutral, but many people would claim that there is an inherent 'bias' for or against a position. Box 3.3 gives one example of how bias operates in the real world.

BOX 3.3 ARE THE MEDIA BIASED?

A poll run by YouGov (Smith, 2018) asked Leave and Remain voters of various ages and across the regions about their perception of bias exhibited by a range of news organisations. See the following article for a representation of this: https://yougov.co.uk/news/2018/02/22/bbc-news-pro-brexit-or-anti-brexit/

While it was clear that some news outlets were perceived to be very much pro-Brexit, e.g. the *Daily Mail* and the *Sun*, some people's perception was quite different, e.g. that the BBC and the *Guardian* were anti-Brexit. If we look deeper at the data, they reveal that the situation was a bit more complex – but isn't it always?

Refer back to the article above for a representation of the data on how people perceived the BBC. If you had asked the same question of people who voted leave and then people who voted remain you would see that only 14% of remainers thought that the BBC was anti-Brexit compared with 45% of leavers. Overwhelmingly what these data do show is that these people, both leave and remain, had no idea whether an organisation was pro- or anti-Brexit. In the case of the broadcast news channels, more people felt that the channels were indeed neutral.

The biggest response was 'don't know', which just goes to show that many people are not necessarily thinking too deeply about the issues covered in the news, and not analysing what those news reports are saying.

Bias is something that researchers should be acutely aware of and that readers of research should also be aware of. As well as actively seeking out instances of researcher bias, you must also guard against your own bias colouring your view of the research.

Forms of bias

There are many forms of bias that can affect research output, and certainly too many to consider in detail here. Essentially, we can group biases into one of four types, i.e. cognitive, social, contextual and statistical. These groupings are not exclusive and certainly not comprehensive. Below are descriptions of the more common biases that present themselves within research or that we may be susceptible to holding (see Table 3.1).

Table 3.1   Categories of common bias

Cognitive Bias	Contextual Bias	Social Bias	Statistical Bias
Anchoring	Academic	Authority	Experimenter
Attribution	Funding	Self-Serving	Reporting
Confirmation			Selection
Framing			
Status Quo			

Cognitive bias

A cognitive bias is really a flaw in logical thinking. A cognitive bias can mean that a person acts in an irrational way, usually based on their own experiences and preferences taking precedence in their decision making. The problem is that it's difficult to recognise your own cognitive biases and you will believe that your decisions are rational and logical even if, to others, they seem not to be. There can also be an element of 'group think' that can aid and abet a cognitive bias. If others you work with think one way or believe that an approach is effective, it's normal for you to join in with the belief rather than stick out and counter that 'group think'. Below are some of the more common cognitive biases explained in more detail.

Anchoring bias

The basis for this bias is an over-reliance on one or a few pieces of research/evidence that 'strikes a chord' when first encountered. In effect, you discount other available evidence, or you are influenced by the initial evidence such that it colours your view of the subsequent evidence you read. This is particularly the case if the evidence matches your instinct (see confirmation bias below). In effect you anchor your decisions and your logical processes on a key piece of evidence or research while ignoring or querying everything else, whether confirmatory or conflicting. Anchoring bias can result in a person making an irrational decision since the first information they encounter sets the baseline for all other decisions. An example of anchoring bias is best illustrated using a classic experiment described by Strack and Mussweiler (1997) where two groups of people were asked to estimate what age Gandhi was when he died. Two improbable statements were used as base references. One group of people was asked if Gandhi died before or after the age of 9 and the second group were asked if he had died before or after the age of 140. The average age at death for the first group was 50, but for the second it was 67. The anchoring points, although factually improbable/impossible, influenced the group's estimation. Gandhi was assassinated at the age of 78.

Attribution bias

In education settings we often look to determine why people behave the way that they do. It can be children, e.g. what causes them to misbehave or to behave, or it could be about the 'behaviour' of teachers, e.g. how they teach, what they do etc. In trying to determine the causes of people's behaviour we can fall foul of attribution bias.

We will often attribute certain behaviours to either personal characteristics or the situations in which people find themselves. When a behaviour is unusual, e.g. when a normally well-behaved child misbehaves, we can be led to attribute the cause to personality or personal traits rather than what may be a simple reason, e.g. that the child has chosen to misbehave, or that sometimes children do naughty things for no good reason.

Another common form of attribution bias is the tendency to attribute success in educational settings to internal factors, and failure to external factors, e.g. thinking that a change in teaching approach is responsible for increased grades, whereas a decrease in grades must be due to other, outside factors such as children's excessive screen time in the home setting. Such bias may also work against teachers. Kennedy (2010 p.591), for example, describes how the observation of teachers by others, including senior leaders, 'may focus too much on the characteristics of teachers themselves, overlooking situational factors that may have a strong bearing on the quality of the teaching practices we see'. Her view is that in order to eliminate attribution bias, we need to change our tacit view of teaching to ensure that 'situation characteristics' are taken into account when evaluating teaching (see Figure 3.1). In her original paper Kennedy simply adds the situation characteristics to the initial teacher characteristics, but it can be argued that the situations can be more complex and may well affect not just the teacher but the pupil, and may even further influence teaching practices.

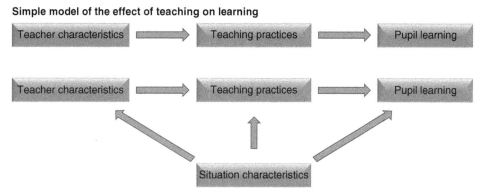

Simple model of the effect of teaching on learning

More realistic model for the effect of teaching on learning

Figure 3.1   Teaching and learning attribution of characteristics and their effects (adapted from Kennedy, 2010)

Confirmation bias

This is probably the most commonly understood bias. Confirmation bias is the tendency to look for and actively seek out research that confirms any pre-existing ideas you may have. It fits with your beliefs and it is linked to a flawed understanding of inductive reasoning. By gathering evidence that confirms your own desired outcome you 'confirm' that your general observations are correct. You should seek to gather evidence and observations that are robust and rigorous regardless of the outcome (i.e. evidence that disproves your belief or idea is just as valuable as evidence that may confirm your belief). The problem with confirmation bias is that it does the opposite of what should be done when testing ideas or hypotheses. In science, the purpose of any research is to try and falsify ideas, i.e. to seek to disprove the idea. Confirmation bias does the opposite – it seeks to prove the idea, and as a result can lull people into a false path where they disregard any falsification and give undue prominence to confirmatory evidence. The term was first described by the psychologist Peter Wason in the 1960s who conducted a simple series of studies to show that people will seek to confirm an idea rather than disprove one (Wason, 1960).

Framing bias

A framing bias is an effect that depends on the way information is presented to people. How information is presented can affect how a person decides whether that information is viewed as positive or negative. For example, when looking at financial information people will usually decide whether it is good or bad depending on whether or not they see it as being a potential profit or loss. Framing bias is very heavily used in marketing (e.g. pushing the positive attributes of a product or the low cost of a product) and within politics. In the 2018 US mid-term elections, the Republican Party used the framing effect in demonising immigrants and asylum seekers by invoking images of fear, crime and violence, whereas the Democrats used the framing effect on healthcare and taxes to try and influence voters. In education, the use of 'mindset' (Dweck, 2012, 2015, 2016) could be argued to be a framing effect in that you are 'framing' the negatives of failure as something that can be seen positively and could lead to success.

Status quo bias

Put simply, this is a fear of change. People generally prefer the *status quo* to having to go through change that may not result in improvement. It is sometimes referred to as 'default bias'. Rather than change, we default to the same choices. This form of bias is seen in many spheres of life – from people who regularly order the same meal or drink choices from menus at restaurants they frequent, to teachers who default to a preferred style of teaching as they believe it is the 'best way'. A problem with status quo bias is the effect it has on preventing the implementation of policy outcomes.

It has been argued that the default philosophy for education has, at its heart, testing (Gunzenhauser, 2003). For example, usually no educational reform is discussed without reference to testing and to how such reforms may influence pupil outcomes with respect to that testing. This is a form of default bias that works at a system level rather than at an individual level. Even if a reform is not aimed at testing, in the form of public examinations, there is usually a measure (or test) that is reported upon. Such a systematic bias can restrict change. As Gunzenhauser (2003 p.51) points out:

> In the current context of schooling, the default philosophy is one that places inordinate value on the scores achieved on high-stakes tests, rather than on the achievement that the scores are meant to represent.

This means that the interpretation of much education research will most likely be within this default philosophy.

Contextual bias

A contextual bias is one where a person can be influenced by extraneous information that is not necessarily relevant. Such a bias can lead to a decision being made that is not wholly justified by the evidence on which it is based. One area where this can be illustrated is in forensic science where evidence is used to determine the guilt or innocence of a person.

BOX 3.4 CONTEXT DRIVES DECISIONS

Many of our decisions are driven by context. A simple example of this would be to think of a word that can fulfil the following pattern: S _ _ P. With no context, the answer you provide could be one of at least three common words, such as SWAP, SOAP or SOUP. If, prior to asking you to complete the word, you were asked about what you had to eat, what sort of foods you enjoy and what's a nice warming food for a cold day, you will be more likely to choose SOUP for your word than SOAP. If the context provided had been how often you shower, whether you use a shower gel, or when you last did some clothes washing, your word is more likely to be SOAP.

The above is a simple example of context-driven bias. In forensic science, context-driven bias is more problematic and could lead to faulty outcomes in a trial.

In a study of forensic scientists who specialised in fingerprint identification, Dror et al. (2006) described some interesting findings. Given two fingerprints, one partial one from a crime scene and one held on file, there was a low rate of 'matching' of the partial print to the one on file. However, once the scientists had been exposed to domain-specific information (i.e. information about the potential suspects and the crime scene) they were more likely to change their minds on whether the two fingerprints matched, leading to a higher match rate.

In a second study, Dror and Hampikian (2011) found that if a forensic scientist was alerted to contextual information about the case by an investigator, such as the existence of a confession, or where the case involved a highly emotional context, such as child killing/abduction, then the forensic scientist could be influenced by the context regardless of whether the scientist was a novice or an experienced practitioner. Dror and colleagues found that this influence could be found even in cases where DNA profiles were being matched to individuals from complex mixed samples (i.e. where the samples contained DNA from the suspect as well as innocent people).

Academic bias

If the beliefs of an academic or researcher drive and shape the research they undertake, this is a form of academic bias. Such bias could affect what is being researched, e.g. the academic may choose to research only things on which they have strong views (either positive or negative). An academic bias may also exist should a researcher choose to include only that evidence which is likely to support their own belief or view (see also confirmation bias).

Funding bias

Who has funded the research is something all academics and researchers should divulge when publishing their research in journals or reports. A funding bias can work in more ways than one. The obvious funding bias is that research delivers a result that in some way is advantageous to the organisation that funded the research. There are some interesting and funny examples of this (see Box 3.5 for one example), which often take the form of news items where a 'scientist' discovers the secret of some mysterious yet frivolous phenomenon.

BOX 3.5 HOW TO RIDE A BIKE

In 2010 it was announced in the national press that scientists had devised a formula to explain how people ride a bike. The announcement went into some detail about inertia, gravity, torque etc. The formula ran to 31 numbers and symbols with 9 sets of brackets.

The key to riding a bike is to ensure that you pedal fast enough so that you don't fall over. The article pointed to research teams from three universities and quoted one of the lead scientists, who brought in Newton's laws of gravity. The giveaway with respect to the research was the timing and the funder. The research was published during National Bike Week and the funder was the bicycle retailer Halfords. This however does not negate the research. The mathematics is sound and the researchers conducted experiments and took measurements. In this example the funder is, naturally, using the result to gain free media exposure to raise awareness of their brand and hopefully sell more bicycles.

The example in the box above does not represent serious funder bias, it was more of a way to market products or advertise. If you carefully read the newspapers at key times of the year it is likely that some company has funded a scientist or mathematician to produce an explanation or formula to promote a product, from chocolate to ice-cream, or, as shown above, a bike. The key point here is to look carefully at any declared interests that researchers provide to ascertain whether any funder bias could be at play.

Another form of funder bias could be the suppression of research or the non-funding of replication studies. Funders of research will naturally be uncomfortable publishing research that has negative outcomes. In research generally, articles with positive or significant outcomes have a greater chance of being published than research that fails to show a positive or significant outcome (Fanelli, 2012). If funded research delivers outcomes that the funder may not wish to be published, it is possible for such research to be supressed. Where government funding has paid for research or reports there have been claims that unfavourable reports have been supressed or simply shelved. In 2016, for example, a report commissioned by the DfE into the viability of small schools providing Universal Free School Meals for Infants was, allegedly, supressed. This led to a freedom of information request to have the report released. Initially this was refused, but an appeal to the Information Commissioner's office overturned that decision and the DfE was ordered to release the report (Dickens, 2016).

Social bias

Social bias can lead to people providing answers to questions that will be favourably viewed by the researcher/questioner. Simply put, they give the answer they think you want to hear. In certain types of research, such as focus groups or group interviews, there is a higher chance of social bias. In group situations people can end up copying or replicating the choices of others in the group. Even in settings where the researcher is observing and recording behaviour, e.g. in a classroom situation, there is always the chance that the observed behaviour is a result of one child/group of children imitating the behaviour of others in the class. A simple remedy for this, you would think, would be to observe behaviour independently of a group. Even this, however, does not eliminate the possibility of social bias. We know that in social contexts people engage in behavioural mimicry, i.e. we tend to copy the behaviours of people with whom we are interacting. This is often an unconscious behaviour which leads to developing a rapport and is a natural way of displaying empathy or increasing likability (Chartrand et al., 2005). What Chartrand et al. also found was that this mimicry also happens in situations that lead to choices. Interestingly, they found that these behaviours not only happened in group situations where the choices could be observed, but also in individual situations. For example, in a supermarket, people choosing wine may well observe the choices of others and choose the same wine. Interestingly, even with those who decide not to choose the same wine while the original person is present (perhaps for fear of being seen to be a 'follower' rather than an independent leader), they will, once the original person leaves, then pick the same wine.

Authority bias

In schools we prefer our pupils to obey our authority. Very few, if any, schools have no rules or no authority figures. In life generally, we have authority figures whom we tend to obey. It may be our GP, who we see as an authority on health matters, or a priest, who we may see as the authority on religious matters. We tend to obey people in authority positions, especially figures such as police officers, or medical or other emergency services. If Prince Charles's personal physician told him to remove his trousers, jump up on an examination couch and stick his bottom up into the air, it is likely he would comply, even if he felt that it would, at best, be undignified and not a position he would ever wish to be seen in by people. We tend to hold doctors etc. as more experienced and knowledgeable. In education the same is true. The teacher is seen to be an authority figure and it is expected that pupils will obey their instructions as they are more knowledgeable and experienced. Researchers can also be seen as authority figures who are more knowledgeable and experienced than teachers generally. An additional factor is the status of the person who may be seen as more authoritative because of their earned title, e.g. Dr or Professor, or an honorary title, e.g. Lady, Dame, Sir, Lord. In recent times also authority has started to be gained by those who have many social media followers, with the number of those followers lending the person a degree of credibility and authority.

One of the most famous examples of authority bias is the experiment carried out by Stanley Milgram in the 1960s. In this experiment Milgram looked at the conflict between authority and personal conscience. The experiments took place during a period when war criminals from the Second World War were being placed on trial. The phrase 'just following orders' implied that authority figures could get lower ranks to perform unspeakable acts – something that would normally be unconscionable (see Box 3.6).

BOX 3.6 THE MILGRAM EXPERIMENT

Milgram wanted to know how far someone would go to obey an instruction if it involved inflicting pain on another. The experiment involved the subject (called the teacher) delivering increasingly higher levels of electrical shocks to another subject (the student), unseen by the teacher. The unseen person could be heard (i.e. sounds of discomfort or pain). The teacher was asked to deliver a small (yet increasing) electrical shock to the unseen student when they provided a wrong answer to a question. If the teacher refused, the experimenter would provide verbal 'prods' to coerce the teacher to continue, e.g. "please continue", "the experiment requires you to continue", up to and including "you have no other choice but to continue".

The result of the experiment, carried out on 40 men from various social backgrounds, aged 20–50, was that two-thirds of them continued to deliver the shocks up to the highest level (450 volts). All of them delivered shocks up to

300 volts. The experiment was, however, a set-up, in that the 'student' was never given an electrical shock and was primed to behave as if he had, and was to consistently provide wrong answers so that the 'teacher' would have to deliver a shock. Milgram explained the results of his experiments in his book (Milgram, 1974 p.2):

> The legal and philosophic aspects of obedience are of enormous import, but they say very little about how most people behave in concrete situations. I set up a simple experiment at Yale University to test how much pain an ordinary citizen would inflict on another person simply because he was ordered to by an experimental scientist.

> Stark authority was pitted against the subjects' strongest moral imperatives against hurting others, and, with the subjects' ears ringing with the screams of the victims, authority won more often than not. The extreme willingness of adults to go to almost any lengths on the command of an authority constitutes the chief finding of the study and the fact most urgently demanding explanation.

Critics of Milgram claim that the original experiments may have lacked 'experimental realism' as the subjects may not have truly believed they were delivering a painful shock to another person. The research was also criticised for presenting a biased sample: it only included men (would women display the same obedience to authority?) and the sample was self-selecting rather than being representative of the population. The subjects had all answered a newspaper advertisement asking for subjects and promising payment for taking part.

Self-serving bias

People tend to attribute positive outcomes to their own hard work. When things go wrong, people often blame others or things that were beyond their control. This is self-serving bias, also known as positivity bias. The opposite can also happen with people who suffer from depression or low self-esteem, i.e. they see a positive event as out of their control and negative events as a result of their own flawed character. A meta-analysis of 266 studies (Mezulis et al., 2004 p.711), confirmed that 'a self-serving attributional bias is pervasive in the general population but demonstrates significant variability across age, culture and psychopathology'.

Statistical bias

Statistical analysis is used to make sense of the data in quantitative research. It is a scientific approach used to analyse numbers so that we can interpret the data gathered and answer research questions. Statistics is essentially the turning of raw numbers into useful information. There are two main branches of statistics, namely descriptive and inferential. 'Descriptive' statistics, as the name implies, tells us about the characteristics of what is being studied. For example, it could describe the number of boys and girls in a school, or the percentage of teachers in different age groups in the schools run by a multi-academy trust. Descriptive statistics provides the majority of information on local, regional or national league tables. Inferential statistics makes inferences (assumptions, suppositions, possibilities) about populations – this may be the population as a whole, or it could be a discrete sub-set of the 'population' such as a specific group or number of schools, e.g. state-maintained schools or academies. Inferential statistics, unlike descriptive statistics, usually has a stated hypothesis (often called the null hypothesis) and an alternative hypothesis (a statement about the relationship between two or more variables). The purpose of producing a null and an alternative hypothesis is to challenge an orthodoxy. The null hypothesis is usually the 'accepted fact', i.e. what we commonly think happens. The alternative hypothesis is another but different explanation. The research is then formulated to challenge or reject the null hypothesis.

There are a number of different types of statistical bias (too many to effectively cover in this chapter), but generally there are three types of bias that can often be identified easily.

Experimenter bias

A difficult but important aspect of research is avoiding experimenter bias – this is also known as the 'observer-expectancy effect'. The construction of research instruments, such as surveys, questionnaires and interviews, should avoid influencing the outcome with subtle (or sometimes not so subtle) questions that would lead the subject to provide an answer that the experimenter would like to see/hear rather than what the subject actually thinks. These are what are commonly known as 'leading questions'. There is an art and a science to composing good questions for use in research that avoid 'leading' those answering the questions to provide the answers the researcher was looking for.

Coercive language used in questions indicates an inherent bias. If questions are posed in such a way that providing a certain answer is surely 'common sense', or what most people would do, then this is a sure sign of experimenter bias.

BOX 3.7 EXAMPLES OF EXPERIMENTER BIAS

Think about the following, simple question:

> *Do you agree that knowledge, rather than skills, is fundamental to a good education?*

Is there any implicit bias in this question? In short, the answer is yes. The question is implying that knowledge is fundamental to a good education, whereas skills are not. The juxtaposition of 'agree' with knowledge (a positive link) and 'rather than' with skills (a negative link) is leading the subject to agree with the statement rather than disagree.

Another form of coercion would be to try to make the respondent feel that agreeing with the premise of the question confers on them a feeling that they are part of a specific group that is, in some ways, intellectually, morally or ethically 'above' others. For example, take the following statement:

> *Experts state that zero-tolerance behaviour management policies lead to improved examination results. Do you agree?*

In this case the subject is being coerced to side with the 'experts' – even though who the experts are is not made explicit – and that 'zero-tolerance' is a position that leads to improvements in examination results. Do those who disagree with the statement feel that they could be viewed as teachers who are not concerned about good discipline and who do not wish to see improvements in results. It is likely that such a statement will elicit a high percentage of teachers who agree with the statement.

Another form of question that is leading or coercive joins two unconnected or minimally connected things suggesting that one will influence the other:

> *Mrs Smith has donated millions of pounds to educational charities. How much confidence do you have in her to lead a newly formed multi-academy trust?*

In this case, the philanthropy of Mrs Smith is unrelated to her ability to lead a multi-academy trust. There is an element of coercion suggesting that because someone donates money to educational charities, he or she must be a 'good' leader. Leadership and management skills have nothing to do with charitable intentions.

Reporting bias

How you report the results of research can be influenced – and therefore a bias introduced – by a range of factors. One factor discussed above is publication bias, where positive or significant results tend to get preferential treatment by being more likely to be published and published quickly. Delaying publication or introducing a specific time lag and publishing results when other, more newsworthy stories exist is a good example of reporting bias. As outlined earlier, funder bias may also play a part.

Selection bias

In any research that purports to have findings that can be generalised, selection of the groups, things or people being studied is key. The participants in any research project may well be quite different from the whole population from which they are drawn. This is similar to the issue of polls (which was looked at in Box 3.2). How do we know that the participants are representative of the population we are studying? If we study the academic achievement of children taking a physics GCSE, but our sample contains a high proportion of boys and these were drawn from schools in Kent where grammar schools are common, it is not a good sample, rather a biased selection. Generally, researchers will be aware of the issues of selection bias and will work hard either to select populations for study that are representative, or acknowledge when a sample is not representative and avoid trying to make generalised findings.

An interesting case of selection bias, not related to education research but which illustrates counterintuitive thinking in experimental design and selection, is described in Box 3.8.

BOX 3.8 IMPROVING SURVIVAL RATES OF AIRCRAFT IN WW2

During the Second World War, the statistician Abraham Wald was set the problem of how to increase the survival rates of aircraft, and more importantly air crew, engaged in battle. The thinking at the time was that aircraft needed more protection in the form of armour plating. Planes that returned to base were inspected, and for those parts where there was evidence of damage from gunfire, protective plating was added. The expectation was that more planes would survive and with them more crew. The result baffled the investigators. Instead of the rate of loss of planes decreasing, it increased. Wald, however, could see a reason for this. He argued that the data about survivability did not come from the damaged parts of the plane, but from the areas that had not sustained damage. His reasoning was that despite being damaged, some planes still made it back to base.

The damage did not cause the plane to crash, so adding extra armour plating in the damaged areas would have little positive effect. On the other hand, the undamaged areas of the returning aeroplanes, if hit by gunfire, may have resulted in it being shot down and the crew killed. Counterintuitively, Wald suggested that those areas only should be given more protection. He realised that simply adding more weight to the planes in areas that were clearly not vital made it less manoeuvrable and slower, and thus more prone to being shot down. The heavier aeroplanes were also less fuel efficient, with a reduced flying range.

Summary

Being organised in your reading brings with it a number of advantages. You can keep track of what you are reading and ensure you stick to reading relevant literature. More importantly, you must have a purpose in mind when reviewing any research literature. If you are conducting your own research, for a dissertation, the literature review is a key chapter. It allows you to identify what is known, and perhaps more importantly what is not known, about a specific concept or subject. Which type of literature review is best suited to your research will very much depend on the research questions you formulate.

While it would be nice to think that all published research is bias free, that is never the case. Knowing and understanding what bias is and how to recognise it will help with your critical analysis of any research reading. All researchers will have an inherent bias. The best are aware of their own biases and will make it clear in their research if there are any underlying assumptions included or any biases present. In this chapter, a range of potential biases has been explored with some real-life examples used to illustrate how those biases are evident in published research and/or reports.

Further reading

Booth, A., Sutton, A., & Papaioannou, D. (2016) *Systematic Approaches to a Successful Literature Review* London: Sage

This book shows you how to take a structured and organised approach to a wide range of literature review types and helps you choose which approach is right for your research. Packed with constructive tools, examples, case studies and hands-on exercises, it covers the full range of literature review techniques.

Torraco, R.J. (2016) Writing integrative literature reviews: using the past and present to explore the future *Human Resource Development Review* Vol.15 No.4 pp.404–428

This article identifies the main components of the integrative literature review, provides examples of visual representations for use in literature reviews, and describes how to write literature reviews that are integrative, definitive, and provocative.

Roulston, K., & Shelton, S.A. (2015) Reconceptualizing bias in teaching qualitative research methods *Qualitative Inquiry* Vol.21 No.4 pp.332–342

This article examines how bias has been understood in qualitative inquiry.

Bibliography

Chartrand, T.L., Maddux, W.W., & Lakin, J.L. (2005) Beyond the perception-behavior link: the ubiquitous utility and motivational moderators of nonconscious mimicry. In Hassin, R.R., Uleman, J.S., & Bargh, J.A. (eds) *The New Unconscious* pp.334–361 New York: Oxford University Press

Dickens, J. (2016) DfE ordered to publish suppressed infant free school meals report [online]. Learning & Skills Events Consultancy and Training Ltd. Available at: https://schoolsweek.co.uk/dfe-ordered-to-publish-suppressed-infant-free-school-meals-viability-report/

Dror, I.E., Charlton, D., & Péron, A.E. (2006) Contextual information renders experts vulnerable to making erroneous identifications *Forensic Science International* Vol.156 No.1 pp. 74–78

Dror, I.E., & Hampikian, G. (2011) Subjectivity and bias in forensic DNA mixture interpretation *Science & Justice* Vol.51 No.4 pp.204–208

Dweck, C. (2012) *Mindset: How You Can Fulfil Your Potential* London: Robinson

Dweck, C. (2015) Carol Dweck revisits the growth mindset *Education Week* Vol.35 No.5 pp.20–24

Dweck, C. (2016) What having a "growth mindset" actually means *Harvard Business Review* 13 pp.213–226

Fanelli, D. (2012) Negative results are disappearing from most disciplines and countries *Scientometrics* Vol.90 No.3 pp.891–904

Gunzenhauser, M.G. (2003) High-stakes testing and the default philosophy of education *Theory Into Practice* Vol.42 No.1 pp.51–58

Kennedy, M.M. (2010) Attribution error and the quest for teacher quality *Educational Researcher* Vol.39 No.8 pp.591–598

Labaree, R.V. (2018) Research Guides: Organizing Your Social Sciences Research Paper: 5. The Literature Review [online]. University of Southern California. Available at: http://libguides.usc.edu/c.php?g=235034&p=1559822

Lather, P. (1993) Fertile obsession: validity after poststructuralism *The Sociological Quarterly* Vol.34 No.4 pp. 673–693

Mezulis, A.H., Abramson, L.Y., Hyde, J.S., & Hankin, B.L. (2004) Is there a universal positivity bias in attributions? A meta-analytic review of individual, developmental, and cultural differences in the self-serving attributional bias *Psychological Bulletin* Vol.130 No.5 p.711

Milgram, S. (1974) *Obedience to Authority: An Experimental View* London: Tavistock

Norris, N. (1997) Error, bias and validity in qualitative research *Educational Action Research* Vol.5 No.1 pp.172–176

Smith, M. (2018) Is BBC News pro-Brexit or anti-Brexit? [online]. YouGov. Available at: https://yougov.co.uk/topics/media/articles-reports/2018/02/22/bbc-news-pro-brexit-or-anti-brexit (accessed November 25th 2018)

Stake, R.E. (1995) *The Art of Case Study Research* London: Sage

Strack, F., & Mussweiler, T. (1997) Explaining the enigmatic anchoring effect: mechanisms of selective accessibility *Journal of Personality and Social Psychology* Vol.73 No.3 pp.437–446

Thomas, G. (2016) *How To Do Your Case Study* (2nd edn) Thousand Oaks, CA: Sage

Wason, P.C. (1960) On the failure to eliminate hypotheses in a conceptual task *Quarterly Journal of Experimental Psychology* Vol.12 No.3 pp.129–140

PART 2
ANALYSING RESEARCH

4
Understanding Research Paradigms

Chapter aims

- Understand the difference between social science research and research in disciplines such as the sciences

- Know what is meant by ontology, epistemology and axiology

- Be familiar with some key social science research paradigms

- Consider the sources of knowledge that inform social science research

Introduction

Education is a social science, which means it is part of the academic discipline that studies society in general and 'the ways in which people behave and influence the world around us' (ESRC (Economic and Social Research Council), 2016). Social sciences cover a range of disciplines from sociology to social anthropology, linguistics, social history and more.

Whatever your original degree subject, you will be reading research within the realm of social science. For some researchers the shift will barely be perceptible, e.g. if they had studied sociology. For others, there will be a major move from one discipline to another, e.g. from the pure/natural sciences to social sciences. Wherever you began your academic career, you will now need to adjust to thinking like a social scientist and take on board the various research methods and methodologies that entails. This chapter will help you understand three essentials for research: understanding and finding out about what the reality is for the object of your research (ontology); figuring out how you know what you know (epistemology); and recognising what your values are in relation to what you are studying (axiology). These things are crucial to understanding the research you are conducting or reading about.

This chapter begins with a short introduction to the problem of moving from one subject discipline to another – in this case moving from a scientific (natural sciences) discipline to a social scientific discipline. It then defines and considers ontological, epistemological and axiological positions, and how these are the foundation of social science research. In the next section, different research paradigms are outlined alongside their key characteristics.

Moving paradigms

Different approaches to research in the social sciences will have overlap, tensions and/or contradictions. Moving from another discipline into working within the social

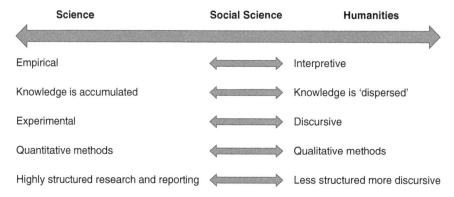

Figure 4.1   Continuum of research approaches (adapted from Coffin et al., 2003)

sciences often entails personal conflict. As Figure 4.1 shows, there are distinct differences between the various academic disciplines when it comes to research.

Box 4.1 contains an account of the transition I made, moving from being a 'scientist' who had originally studied a natural science discipline (geology), to studying and researching education – a major discipline in social science.

BOX 4.1 A SCIENTIST OPERATING IN THE SOCIAL SCIENCES

> I want to understand the world from your point of view. I want to know what you know in the way you know it. I want to understand the meaning of your experience, to walk in your shoes, to feel things as you feel them, to explain things as you explain them. Will you become my teacher and help me understand? (Spradley, 1979 p.34)

The quotation above reflects the main difficulty I had with qualitative research. I needed someone to help me move from being a scientist to understanding social science. As a scientist who had previously studied geology, the key issues I needed to address were objectivity and bias – the unintentional introduction of any bias I may have had on the data I gathered, or even the gathering process itself, and the possible lack of objectivity in the interpretation of any generated data.

Scientists as positivists

The natural sciences are often thought to operate on purely observational and quantitative levels. It is often assumed that the scientist exists independently of the idea/concept/material/phenomenon being investigated. In effect, the scientist normally stands on the outside looking in and does try to interact with what it is they are studying. The evidence for scientists comes from sense data derived from natural phenomena. This position and view of scientific research is often referred to as a 'positivist' view that uses empirical data.

Researchers in the sciences prefer quantitative measures as the basis for the determination of the results of experiments. They are, in this respect, also realists, though as it will be explained later, science has moved on from being strictly positivist. The idea of 'being' part of the research, being an 'insider', is particularly uncomfortable for many scientists. The idea that they may interact with their subject and could materially change what's happening means that instinctively there is a distrust of social science research in the eyes of the scientist as they do not see it as truly 'objective'. There are also issues about rigour and generalisability. A goal of science is to explain nature, or more specifically,

(Continued)

to explain natural phenomena, and as such to make those explanations apply widely.

In a lot of educational research, what is reported has to be seen in the context within which the research was done. Moving from being a scientist to a social scientist means leaving behind aspects of scientific rigour and learning to view the world in a different way.

Positivists assume a reality exists and use a scientific approach (a 'scientific method') to uncover and explain that reality. For positivists/realists, a particular issue with a qualitative approach is the lack of generalisability of results, but we need to remember that the object of qualitative research is understanding, rather than causal determination, which is often a goal in the natural sciences.

If you are moving from one discipline to another, you will need to reflect on your own understanding of how research is carried out in the new discipline. It is useful to reflect on the following:

- your academic background;
- how you have carried out research in the past, or how new you are to research;
- the difficulties you anticipate in moving from your original academic background to the field of social science.

The move to post-positivist/critical realism

Strict positivism has its problems. One of the main issues is the idea that by studying the world scientifically we can know and understand everything. In positivism, sense data (i.e. things we can – using our senses – observe, touch etc.) provide the evidence that will lead us to some form of 'truth' about the world in which we live. This falls down when we try to explain things that we cannot sense directly – for example, how do we know that a sub-atomic particle exists if we cannot see it? Directly we cannot see an atom or an electron with our eyes. Even using instruments, it's very difficult if not impossible. We can infer their existence from their effects, e.g. we can infer that electrons exist, as a flow of electrons produces an electric current. We can measure the current and infer the rate of flow. Strict positivism then has issues.

To help resolve this, many scientists would now describe themselves as post positivists using a philosophy called critical realism.

A critical realist accepts that there is a reality and that this reality exists independently from our thoughts. Post-positivist critical realists accept that any observation and much sense data can be fallible. For example, if you talk to three witnesses of a road accident they will rarely agree on the detail of what each of them had seen (a fuller explanation of this is provided in the Introduction). Critical realists also recognise that in science, while a theory is 'as good as it gets', theories are not fixed and unchanging. Theories can, and do, get revised as new evidence informs the explanations scientists form as theory. Critical realists, unlike positivists, do not strive to uncover the truth using the methods of science, they are really looking to find the best explanation for phenomena. Critical realists understand that a perfect description of reality that holds truth in all cases will never be achieved. Even the most precise and accurate measurements will have a degree of uncertainty – it may be a very small degree of uncertainty, but no measurement or sense data can ever be 'true'. In a bid to reduce the error and uncertainty, post-positivist critical realists will use *triangulation* as a way of increasing certainty, i.e. confirming the evidence or data using three or more different sources.

Thinking about the '-ologies'

The suffix '-ology' simply means 'the study of'. Biology, for example, is the study of living things, and geology the study of the earth. The original meaning of 'science' is knowledge (of anything). We tend to restrict the definition of 'scientist' to those who study the natural sciences, but the suffix 'science' is used quite liberally for disciplines that are not natural sciences, such as political science, library science etc. Sociology (the study of society and of human social interaction) is a social science, and like natural sciences has a few '-ologies' that need explaining.

Ontology and ontological perspectives on research

Ontology, or the philosophical study of what exists, and ultimately what that means (O'Leary, 2014; Byrne, 2017), is the initial framing point for most research. Ontology is part of metaphysics and comes under the umbrella of philosophy. It simply asks the question 'What exists?'.

Two very big ontological questions are 'Does God exist?' and 'Does free will exist?'. If we determine that something exists, then ontology is the study of that which we believe exists. The problem with ontology is a fundamental one of existence. Whether we believe something exists or not, how do we know that what we believe to be real is in fact real and does exist? Richard Dawkins will almost certainly state that God does not exist, yet the Archbishop of Canterbury and the Pope may well disagree. The *Stanford Encyclopedia of Philosophy* (Hofweber, 2004) describes ontology as being a discipline with four separate parts:

- the study of ontological commitment, i.e. what we or others are committed to;
- the study of what there is;
- the study of the most general features of what there is, and how these things relate to each other in metaphysical ways;
- the study of meta-ontology, i.e. saying what task it is that the discipline of ontology should aim to accomplish (if any), how the questions it aims to answer should be understood, and with what methodology they can be answered.

In understanding educational research, we only really need to consider the second point – the study of what there is. While some researchers may question the nature of reality, for the purposes of our everyday lives and work, we tend to take a view that a reality exists and that the 'things' we wish to study also exist. The study of ontology itself is highly theoretical and goes beyond the scope of this book. When you review educational research, you need to have some form of ontological commitment that the 'thing' being researched and written about does in fact exist. If you are not convinced that it does and the researcher has not convinced you that the 'thing' exists, then your view of the research will be highly negatively influenced by that.

Epistemology and epistemological perspectives on research

Epistemology is a study of the nature, sources and limits of knowledge (O'Leary, 2014; Byrne, 2017). In short, epistemology is how we know what we know. There is more than one epistemological position that can be held. The normative position is that where we have a particular belief we should judge the reasons for our beliefs, and if those reasons are sound (logical) we may then consider our beliefs to be 'knowledge'. A second, naturalistic position holds that what we need to understand are the conditions under which beliefs can be considered as 'true'. There is an application of scientific 'method' to judging the conditions under which a belief may be held to be true. Once it has been established that the beliefs and conditions are true, only then can we define the beliefs as knowledge (Klein, 2005 p.224). In other words, it is not enough to simply reason that a belief that is held is true and *ipso facto* it becomes knowledge. There must be a reliable source, which is subject to scientific scrutiny, in order to consider that a belief is true. Only then can we consider this belief to be knowledge.

Axiology and axiological perspectives on research

Axiology, or value theory as it is sometimes known, considers the nature of value and what things have value (Frey, 2018). Value in this sense could be aesthetic (beauty) or ethical (right or wrong). Value can also simply mean that something is 'of interest'.

Another aspect of axiology is the way in which the research is conducted, i.e. is it value-free or value-laden? The role of axiology within a research paradigm is important. In strict positivism, for example, research should be done in a value-free way, with scientific objectivity and the researcher looking in from the outside. In social science research, the values of the researcher can influence how data are interpreted. There would be an acknowledged bias that the researcher is influenced by their own worldview, experiences etc. If the researcher is part of what is being researched and cannot easily detach themselves, the outcome will be more subjective than objective.

How knowledge can come from various sources

When we read education research, we are sometimes looking at new knowledge, or different interpretations of existing knowledge. Whatever our ontological, epistemological and axiological positions, we must consider the source of the knowledge we are utilising in our research.

For a natural scientist who is a positivist or post positivist, sense data, i.e. the things we can perceive, that we are directly aware of, are the main source of knowledge. In addition to what can be observed directly, what we can measure or observe with the help of instrumentation (microscopes and telescopes, thermometers and myriad other instruments) will contribute to our knowledge of whatever it is we are studying.

For the social sciences we can gather data in many ways, often separated into qualitative and quantitative. Natural sciences prefer quantitative data, i.e. the things we can measure and record in number form. This allows us to perform various mathematical 'tests' to enable us to come to conclusions about the data and what they tell us. Qualitative data are more favoured by social scientists. In some ways there are links to how social scientists view the world (often somewhat differently from natural scientists), but qualitative data may be the best way to gain 'knowledge' about complex situations that cannot easily be measured and quantified.

At this point it's worth considering the methodological and theoretical approaches to social science research and how these influence the methods chosen by a researcher. There are numerous theoretical approaches that can be taken, and this is just one of the many issues we have when it comes to how we interpret research findings. It was noted a long time ago that despite the existence of many theoretical approaches to research, there remain inconsistencies in the way the terminology used by researchers is defined (Crotty, 1998). There is a relationship between the theoretical approaches, methodology and the methods used in social science research. Understanding these is crucial to interpreting research.

Contrary to the ideas of many students conducting research for the first time, the wrong way to approach a research plan is to start with the methods and build from there. You should begin with your ontological perspective, understand your epistemological perspective, take account of your axiological position, and then choose a methodological approach that fits with these standpoints. From this point you can select the relevant and best methods available to answer your research question(s).

Research paradigms

There are many different research paradigms and the term itself can have a fluidity in its meaning (see Box 4.2). Some researchers tend to use the term 'theoretical framework' interchangeably with 'research paradigm'. The term 'paradigm' was used by the philosopher of science Thomas Kuhn to refer to a particular worldview. A paradigm in Kuhn's view is a way of viewing the world and a framework from which to understand human experience (Kuhn, 1996).

BOX 4.2 THOMAS KUHN'S SCIENTIFIC PARADIGMS

A paradigm can be thought of as a set of ideas or concepts that constitute a belief or worldview that will guide a researcher ontologically and methodologically. The original idea of a paradigm came from the work of the physicist, historian and philosopher of science, Thomas Kuhn (1922–1996).

Before we examine what a 'paradigm' is within a social science context, we need to understand how Kuhn structured his argument and defined a paradigm. In his seminal book *The Structure of Scientific Revolutions*, Kuhn (1996) does not provide a single and consistent definition of what he means by 'paradigm'. Looking at the term holistically, we can conceive of his original paradigm as an inter-connecting matrix of ideas and concepts, theories and models that explain the world in a scientific sense.

Kuhn looked at how scientists behave when faced with the various paradigms that describe the phenomena they study. Scientists (regardless of discipline), he argued, work within these paradigms. The paradigms constitute what Kuhn called 'normal science'. The scientists working within these paradigms tend to be governed by their view of the paradigm. They construct arguments within the existing paradigm.

A frequent issue for scientists is how to deal with anomalies – those results that do not fit the standard explanations that they have. If the anomalies are small and infrequent, then with small adjustments to the prevailing ideas and explanations (theories) they may be accommodated or incorporated. Larger or multiple unexplained anomalies may present a test of the prevailing paradigm.

In this instance, an accumulation of evidence that challenges the prevailing orthodoxy – the prevailing paradigm – can lead to what Kuhn called 'scientific revolutions'. One such revolution was the move from the idea that life on earth was the result of separate creations by God to one that saw the development and diversity of life being explained by natural selection, Darwin and Wallace's theory of evolution published in 1858. Another scientific revolution was the shift from Newtonian physics to the physics of Albert Einstein.

A scientific revolution does not necessarily mean the wholesale replacement and rejection of previous explanations (Newton's Laws of Motion still hold firm, for example) as the old and the new can co-exist. Over time, however, such scientific revolutions represent scientific progress.

Paradigms in social science

Kuhn was not keen on the use of his scientific paradigms within the social sciences. The introduction to his book explains that he viewed scientific paradigms as a mechanism for differentiating between the social and natural sciences (Kuhn, 1996).

Within the natural sciences, there is an element of prediction that can, and indeed should, characterise science. Understanding a natural phenomenon should lead to the ability to predict outcomes. In meteorology for example, predictions were notoriously poor before we had satellites and instruments that could track weather systems in real time. Today meteorologists are able, with varying degrees of success and depending on how far in advance predictions are made, to make reasonably accurate predictions of weather conditions.

Social sciences are somewhat different. While the goal of social science may be ultimately the same as that of science, i.e. understanding, social sciences will not be good at predicting human behaviour. The best we can say is that the gathering and analysis of data in social sciences increases our understanding of society, and while it can never allow a sociologist to predict events, we will have a more sophisticated explanation of events today when compared to our explanations of events 60 years ago (Babones, 2016).

Four popular research paradigms are outlined in Table 4.1. In each case the paradigm is described with reference to any ontological, epistemological and axiological considerations. Taken together these frameworks are often the setting for social science research. Any outcomes or results of such research must be seen in the context of the framing paradigm.

Table 4.1   Mapping research paradigms against fundamental beliefs (adapted from Wahyuni, 2012)

Fundamental Belief	Popular Social Science Research Paradigms			
	Positivism	Post-Positivism (critical realism)	Interpretivism (constructivism)	Pragmatism
Ontology	'Old style' scientific approach to research Aims to be highly objective, independent of society and describes the real world	An objective approach that accepts reality exists independently of human thought Does not assume that all 'laws' of nature can be explained simply through scientific investigation	Defines reality as a human construct, and as such there will be multiple interpretations and multiple 'realities' that can be constructed	While there are multiple views of reality, the one chosen is that which will best provide an answer to the research question No single view of reality is dominant
Epistemology	Data come from what can be observed It assumes that there is a reality independent of our conception of reality and that we can describe that reality and explain it through the use of scientific investigation utilising a 'scientific method'	Critical realism bridges the gap between a scientific positivist approach and a social science approach	The views and opinions of the research participants (researcher and those taking part in the research) form what is known about reality It is an inductive approach	A chief characteristic of pragmatism is a mixed methods approach to answer the problem or question at hand
Axiology	Value-free research where the researcher is 'outside looking in', and the data are gathered independently and objectively with the elimination of bias	It acknowledges that as humans we may have an influence on what we research, and it does not seek to eliminate the subjective	This is a heavily value-laden approach and the researcher is embedded within the research It has a high degree of subjectivity	This is also a value-laden approach, though researchers claim it can be objective as well as subjective depending on the methods used

(This table is not intended as a guide to all possible social science research paradigms. Other equally valid paradigms exist, e.g. critical theory, postmodernism, feminism, transformism. The four represented here are the four most likely to coincide with common research paradigms.)

Education research and the search for 'what works'

There have been calls for better research approaches in the field of education than the dominant interpretivist approaches. Torgerson and Torgerson (2001 p.316), for example, called for a move away from interpretivist approaches to randomised controlled trials (RCTs):

> The dominant paradigm in educational research is based on qualitative methodologies (interpretive paradigm). This is because there are complex interactive processes operating within the classroom situation requiring investigation and understanding.

The call for RCTs was repeated in 2011, this time in a more high-profile way, by Ben Goldacre, a prominent media personality and medical research expert, with the backing of the then Secretary of State for Education, Michael Gove. The aim was to try and improve the quality of research and to enable those in the front line of teaching to be more accepting of such research. Alongside this was a desire to distinguish between 'what works' in education and what does not (Goldacre, 2011; Haynes et al., 2012).

In medicine, for example, there is a strong and veracious adherence to randomised controlled trials to test the effectiveness of a range of medical interventions, from new drugs to new treatment regimes. The argument that we should try to replicate this in education research is attractive. The Education Endowment Foundation (EEF), set up by Former Secretary of State for Education Michael Gove, with £125 million of DfE funding via the Sutton Trust, seeks to provide reliable research and test the claims of education research (Menter, 2013).

Qualitative approaches to any investigation will have limitations, and this can lead to problems with validity and reliability. Ideally, as within the natural sciences, any approach used by a researcher should be able to be reproduced. This, in turn, enhances the validity of the research. In scientific experiments, 'reproducibility' is a term that is often used without a specific definition of what that means. Is it trying to reproduce the method or the results? As Goodman et al. (2016 p.1) report:

> As the movement to examine and enhance the reliability of research expands, it is important to note that some of its basic terms—reproducibility, replicability, reliability, robustness, and generalizability—are not standardized. This diverse nomenclature has led to confusion, both conceptual and operational, about what kind of confirmation is needed to trust a given scientific result.

Given that in a reproduced qualitative study the same subjects may not be involved, it is highly unlikely that the same results will be found. This may also be the case if the reproduced research is conducted by a different researcher, i.e. the same interpretation may not be applied.

The methods of investigation used by a quantitative researcher will be independent (or should be) of any bias of interpretation; however, no research will be bias free and even 'facts' or theories will be value-laden to a certain extent in natural science research. Complete objectivity in any research is a difficult thing to achieve, and while the natural sciences may claim objectivity they are unlikely to achieve this (Reiss and Sprenger, 2014).

A qualitative researcher is often, if not always, a part of the research. He or she may, or may not, declare a bias or share an overarching concept of what is being studied with those involved in the study. The researcher then cannot be independent of the research and may, to some degree or another, influence that research. As a reader of research, you have to ascertain what degree of bias or what assumptions may be made by the researcher.

As stated earlier, a goal of qualitative research (perhaps all research) is understanding, but an understanding of what? This has to be determined from the outset with an explanation of the 'thesis' being put forward. In this sense the term 'thesis' is being used as a statement or idea that is put forward as a premise to be maintained or proved.

While much research is aimed at finding out 'what works', we must acknowledge that any form of intervention could lead to something that 'works' or appears to show an effect. The question is whether the intervention continues to work beyond the initial measured effect.

BOX 4.3 THE HAWTHORNE EFFECT

The Hawthorne factory just outside Chicago, Illinois, was a US factory making various electrical components for Western Electric. In the 1920s a series of experiments were undertaken to measure how changing conditions in the factory affected worker production rates. Investigations were measured against various changes such as keeping workstations clean, clearing work areas of potential obstacles, and changing lighting levels. Usually the latter change is the one most people associate with the Hawthorne effect. In essence, the studies appear to show that changes to working conditions can lead to short-lived changes in productivity. Cleaner workstations improved productivity, and one of the more surprising changes showed that increasing light levels, even by a minimal amount, could also lead to improved productivity.

It wasn't until the results were re-analysed in the late 1950s that the true cause of the changes in worker productivity was identified. The new interpretation postulated that the effect was not the result of the change in conditions so much as the fact that the workers knew that they were being observed for productivity, and as a result were more likely to be productive rather than be seen as less productive which could, in theory, have put their job at risk.

There is debate over whether or not the Hawthorne effect is a real effect. Much of the original data have been lost, though the data from the illumination experiments were re-discovered in 2011. When this was re-analysed, only a modest effect was found (Levitt and List, 2011). The Hawthorne effect continues to be discussed, debated and investigated to this day.

Regardless of the reality (or not) of the Hawthorne effect, the real question to ask here is not 'What works?' but 'What continues to work?' after the initial effects of any intervention could be reasonably expected to have worn off.

The complexity of education

Studying anything to do with teaching and learning raises the issue of complexity. Human interactions are complex. When you put a teacher in a room with 30 children, the interactions soon become so complex that trying to work out what works and what does not seems almost impossible. Replication is also an issue. No two teachers teach the same way, and no two classes behave the same way. Even the same class of children will be different on different days. The web of complexity that exists in the classroom serves almost to defeat description, yet many research papers published make claims about the efficacy of one approach over another. Teachers themselves will debate at length what 'works', and will share resources and tips for better teaching and what is, in their view, ultimately better learning.

Research as a journey of discovery

Any research project is a journey of discovery. All journeys should have a map to guide the traveller. A research paradigm is the worldview that the researcher has. It is how they see the world, how they perceive reality, and how, for the researcher, they arrive at the 'truth' of any given situation. The methodology and methods provide the route map for the research and how the researcher aims to get from 'A' to 'B', from the question to the answer. As with any journey or route map, different researchers will have different ways in which they undertake their journey, but they will all have the common goal of getting to 'B', i.e. the answer. As with journeys in real life, there are no correct or incorrect ways of getting to your destination – some will be routes that have been well travelled and as such they will be well-known and easy to navigate, whereas other routes could result in barriers that cannot be overcome, so as a researcher you may have to double back and change your route. Some journeys will take longer and will be more complex. Ultimately you will know whether the journey is a success when you have an answer that can be supported by evidence. In real life you will know when you have arrived at your destination, as the address you had and the address you have physically arrived at are the same. The route map for research is described by the methodology and methods the researcher uses.

BOX 4.4 A GEOLOGICAL ANALOGY FOR RESEARCH

Reality is multi-layered and has a history. It is, in effect, stratified, much like the exposed face of a cliff. To use a geological fieldwork analogy, as we expose different strata of reality, what we are uncovering is how reality has changed

(Continued)

over time and how previous strata are foundational to the newer strata. The danger is in exposing a single stratum and assuming that this exposed surface tells us all we need to know about the whole cliff (reality). In geological terms, a single stratum of rock will tell you a lot about a particular and specific isolated point in time. You can learn much about the conditions under which the layer of rock was deposited, and depending on its age and composition, you can also learn about the prevailing atmosphere, its site of deposition, perhaps even aspects of the range and type of lifeforms that existed. It will not tell you about any other point in history, about the overlying or underlying strata. These need to be seen and examined separately. Only then can you gain a holistic picture of the multiple realities that make up the cliff exposure.

Methodology and methods in social science research

The difference between methodology and methods can often confuse people new to research. Methodology is the overall approach you take in your research. In effect, it is your research plan or map. It drives and describes the system of methods for the research and sets out how that research was accomplished. The methods describe in detail exactly how it was carried out, how the data were gathered and what tools were used for the research, such as surveys, interviews, observations etc. A researcher's methodological approach will, in effect, reflect the research paradigm, and this in turn can influence the choice of methods used.

In research the methodology section of any paper or article explains how the researcher collected the data. The methods chosen by a researcher will affect their interpretations and findings. Knowing this allows the reader to have a view on how reliable the findings of any research are. It can help to determine whether or not the findings are context bound, i.e. that they only apply in the particular context within which the research was set, or whether they can be 'generalised', i.e. they could apply more widely.

Knowing the research paradigm, the methodology and which methods were used for any research can provide the reader with clues about reliability. Understanding the particular method(s) used for gathering data (either qualitative or quantitative) tells the reader something about the quality of the evidence. For example, if the method was multiple choice questions, were the choices on offer reasonable? Were they comprehensive? Did they 'force' a choice in any way? In a situation where interview data are being used, were the questions asked by the researcher loaded or leading in any way? Did they allow the participant to qualify their answer? How did supplementary questions work? Were the same general questions asked of all participants? You will need to know that the way in which any and all data were collected was consistent with the generally accepted practice in the field of social science research.

Other aspects of the methodology and methods used will be helpful in ascertaining whether the way in which the research was conducted could result in providing evidence to answer the questions asked. If surveys were used, for example, how were participants selected? What was the overall sample size? Can the researchers show that the results can be generalised and represent the views of the population being studied?

A good methodological approach to research will also provide information about any anticipated or actual problems encountered. In addition, how any anticipated issues were controlled or minimised needs to be explained. Chapter 5 will look at the main research methods used in social science research.

Summary

How do we know what we know? How do we find out about the reality we experience and what values do we have and apply to the things we study? These questions set out the epistemological, ontological and axiological aspects of any research we do. When reading research we need to understand what the researcher's views on these things are.

Getting to grips with the various research paradigms under which education research can be conducted is not easy. It is, however, vital to understand the various paradigms and to know which paradigm is your preferred one. If you are going to critically read, review and analyse research it also matters that you understand these fundamental aspects of research. Our knowledge of any situation can come from various sources. How reliable that knowledge is and how we deal with it is important. Interventions in education practice, and then researching the effect of those interventions, may not be a simple cause and effect. As the Hawthorne studies showed, things may change, and indeed improve, simply because people know they are being observed or that an intervention is 'supposed' to have an effect.

Education is complex because people are complex. Finding out what works and does not work in teaching and learning is no less complex. Unlike many scientific experiments where variables may be controlled, the complexity of interacting variables in teaching, learning and within the environments of schools almost defies the notion of 'controls'. We must not be defeatist about research in education, but we must be realistic. Rarely will we find one answer that can be universally applied that is guaranteed to work every time. We should, perhaps, see such a lack of universality in how to teach or how children learn as an opportunity to explore many and varied ways of constructing learning environments.

Further reading

Hyslop-Margison, E.J. (2010) Scientific paradigms and falsification: Kuhn, Popper, and problems in education research *Educational Policy* Vol.24 No.5 pp.815–831

This article argues that identified problems in so-called scientifically designed education research effectively reduce many emergent claims to the realm of logically invalid hypotheses and questionable circumstantial evidence.

Toma, J. (2006) Approaching rigor in applied qualitative research. In Conrad, C.F., & Serlin, R.C. (eds) *The SAGE Handbook for Research in Education* (pp. 405–423) Thousand Oaks, CA: Sage

In contrast to the above article, this book chapter argues that qualitative research can be as rigorous as scientific research. It is, argues the author, simply different but can be as valuable as quantitative research methods.

Wilson, E. (ed.) (2017) *School-based Research: A Guide for Education Students* London: Sage

This book is aimed at new classroom researchers and those studying graduate-level education courses. It contextualises methodological issues within various contexts that school-based researches are concerned with, such as pupil behaviour, attainment grouping etc.

Bibliography

Babones, S. (2016) Interpretive quantitative methods for the social sciences *Sociology* Vol.50 No.3 pp.453–469

Byrne, D. (2017) *Philosophy of Research* London: Sage

Coffin, C., Curry, M.J., Goodman, S., et al. (2003) *Teaching Academic Writing: A Toolkit for Higher Education* Abingdon: Routledge

Crotty, M. (1998) *The Foundations of Social Research*. London: Sage

ESRC (Economic and Social Research Council) (2016) What is social science? [online] http://www.esrc.ac.uk/about-us/what-is-social-science/ (accessed October 26th 2016)

Frey, B.B. (2018) *The SAGE Encyclopedia of Educational Research, Measurement, and Evaluation* Thousand Oaks, CA: Sage

Goldacre, B. (2011) How can you tell if a policy is working? Run a trial | Ben Goldacre [online]. *@guardian*. Available at: http://www.theguardian.com/commentisfree/2011/may/14/bad-science-ben-goldacre-randomised-trials (accessed May 25th 2016)

Goodman, S.N., Fanelli, D. & Ioannidis, J.P.A. (2016) What does research reproducibility mean? *Science Translational Medicine* Vol.8 No.341 pp.1–12

Haynes, L., Service, O., Goldacre, B., & Torgerson, D. (2012) Test, Learn, Adapt: Developing Public Policy with Randomised Controlled Trials [online] Available at: http://papers.ssrn.com/abstract=2131581http://papers.ssrn.com/sol3/Delivery.cfm?abstractid=2131581 (accessed September 22nd 2014)

Hofweber, T. (2004) Logic and Ontology [online] Available at: https://plato.stanford.edu/entries/logic-ontology/ (accessed October 3rd 2017)

Klein, P.D. (2005) Epistemology. In Craig, E. (ed.) *Shorter Routledge Encyclopaedia of Philosophy* pp.224–227 Abingdon: Routledge

Kuhn, T.S. (1996) *The Structure of Scientific Revolutions* (3rd edn) Chicago, IL: University of Chicago Press

Levitt, S.D., & List, J.A. (2011) Was there really a Hawthorne effect at the Hawthorne plant? An analysis of the original illumination experiments *American Economic Journal: Applied Economics* Vol.3 No.1 pp.224–238

Menter, I. (2013) From interesting times to critical times? Teacher education and educational research in England *Research in Teacher Education* Vol.3 No.1 pp.38–40

O'Leary, Z. (2014) *The Essential Guide to Doing Your Research Project* London: Sage

Reiss, J., & Sprenger, J. (2014) Scientific Objectivity [online] Available at: http://plato.stanford.edu/entries/scientific-objectivity/ (accessed May 22nd 2016)

Spradley, J.P. (1979) *The Ethnographic Interview* Belmont, CA: Wadsworth

Torgerson, C.J., & Torgerson, D.J. (2001) The need for randomised controlled trials in educational research *British Journal of Educational Studies* Vol.49 No.3 pp.316–328

Wahyuni, D. (2012) The research design maze: Understanding paradigms, cases, methods and methodologies *Journal of Applied Management Accounting Research* Vol. 10 No. 1 pp. 69-80

5
Research Methods – An Overview

Chapter aims

- Understand the concept of the 'hourglass model' for research
- Be aware of and understand the main categories of logical reasoning
- Define and compare qualitative and quantitative approaches to research
- Understand the main methods used in education research

Introduction

The aim of this chapter is not to describe in detail the various methods used in social science research, as there are many textbooks you can use to learn how to deploy different methods to gather data for research (see Further reading). This chapter summarises the commonest methods used in social science research designs, and more importantly discusses the strengths and weaknesses of the different methods used in different forms of research.

How data are collected generally falls into two different categories: experimental and interpretive. Research utilising such data is referred to as being empirical. At the heart of any research is the use of logic to come to reasoned conclusions. In this chapter the three main types of logic will be examined: deductive, inductive and abductive. Two categories of research will be explored, qualitative and quantitative, and these will be defined and compared. This is followed by an overview of the main methods utilised in social science research and their strengths and weaknesses.

Research designs

All published research will have at its heart a plan that outlines what the question being researched is, and the methods or techniques used to gather the data necessary to answer the specified research questions. A good research design is like a blueprint. The plan should be sufficiently detailed, such that another researcher could, by following the plan, reproduce the research. In science it may consist of details of experiments that could be reproduced. In social science there may be experiments or, more likely, surveys, questionnaires etc. that will generate data. A typical research project follows what's known as the 'hourglass model' (see Box 5.1 and Figure 5.1).

BOX 5.1 THE HOURGLASS MODEL OF RESEARCH

The start of any research encompasses a broad range of ideas, questions and interests. This poses the first problem, i.e. homing in on what the exact subject of the research will be. A major problem for novice researchers is wanting to research too much – too many questions or related issues. For example, if your initial question and interest is 'How do children learn?', this is a very broad area that encompasses many variables. Whole books have been written on this topic and no single piece of research could ever hope to answer the question in full. A lifetime of research may not be enough to answer such a question.

The researcher must narrow the question down to one that can be studied in a research project that considers the resources, time and expertise required. Usually, he or she will produce several focus questions that will cover specific aspects of children's learning, and from there perhaps develop a hypothesis or home in on a specific aspect of learning.

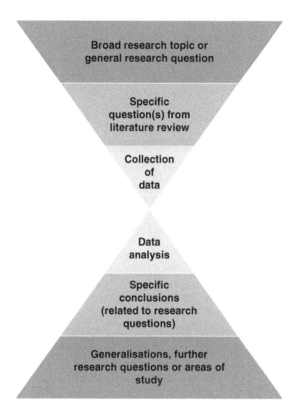

Figure 5.1   The research hourglass

Having conducted a literature review to see what is already known, and where gaps in knowledge exist, the research gets further refined and narrowed down. By this point the project is heading towards the narrowest point of the hourglass. The measurement, observation and data collection phase is analogous to the narrowest point of an hourglass. Datum point by datum point (grain by grain), it passes through the researcher's hands ready to be analysed and interpreted.

(Continued)

After the analysis is complete, the researcher combines the results to build up explanations and interpretations. Essentially, the researcher is trying to understand and make sense of what has been gathered. The process of generating explanations of the data post analysis broadens the researcher's understanding.

The final stage is once more to look at the original broader question and begin the process of generalising. In turn, this may lead to other related questions that emerge from the research process – a further period of broadening. The hourglass is then 'complete'.

Once there is an established methodology (see Chapter 4), the methods should support this overarching framework and generate data that can answer the research questions set out.

Research designs may be wholly experimental (usually quantitative), wholly interpretive (usually qualitative), or may utilise elements of both (commonly known as a 'mixed methods' approach). To understand what the 'experimental' and 'investigative' approaches entail, we need to consider the part that logic plays within any research.

Logic and research

Any research should have reasoned conclusions. The findings derived from an analysis of the data must be logical. Two key forms of logic applied to research are deductive and inductive reasoning. We can broadly relate these forms of reasoning to the two main research designs, i.e. experimental and interpretive. At the heart of both forms of reasoning is theory. The difference between the two is how theory is placed within the reasoning process (see Figures 5.2 and 5.3). A third form of reasoning, also described as 'inference to the best explanation', is abductive reasoning.

Deductive reasoning

In deductive reasoning (see Figure 5.2), the researcher determines the specific from the general. The researcher begins with a generalised theory about an idea or concept, and then designs research that will seek to confirm (or deny) that the theory is correct. This form of reasoning is best applied within experimental settings. In the natural sciences, for example, experiments can be designed and carried out to ascertain whether or not a scientific theory is correct. This process is also known as 'falsification', coming from the work of Karl Popper (see Box 5.2). In his philosopher of science view, science exists not to prove that something is true, but to test our ideas and explanations (theories).

The more a theory is tested and not falsified, the more robust that theory becomes. For Popper, science is not about trying to prove that ideas are true, it is about trying to prove ideas wrong, with any failure to do this strengthening the theory.

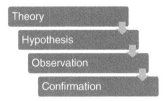

Figure 5.2   Deductive reasoning

BOX 5.2 POPPER'S FALSIFICATION

Karl Popper (1902–1994) was a physicist and philosopher of science. He set out to solve a problem: how to distinguish between scientific and non-scientific theories, a problem called 'demarcation'. Popper argued that for a theory to be considered scientific it must be falsifiable, i.e. there must be a test that could disprove the theory. He wanted a way of determining whether or not something could be scientific that differed from the idea of 'verifiability' which, in the early 20th century, held that something is only meaningful if it can be verified. The problem with verification is that many statements are capable of verification even though the statement may be considered non-scientific. For example, the statement 'goblins are real' is capable of being verified. Although we may never have seen a goblin, there may be a location in the world where a goblin could exist. Just because nobody happens to have been at this location at the same time as a goblin does not mean that goblins do not exist. We may have been unlucky and unable at the present time to verify the existence of goblins. The principle that the existence of goblins could still be verified, however, continues to be true. On the other hand, other statements that are much more realistic would be dismissed as unscientific (unverifiable) as there is no hope of ever being able to conclusively verify it, e.g. the statement 'all swans are white'. While you may count 1,000 swans and determine that every swan so far is white, it would not be possible to verify the statement conclusively at that point. You would need to count and note the colour of every swan that currently existed, determine the colour of every swan that has ever existed, and continue to log the colour of every future swan. What Popper realised is that while verification has considerable problems as a means of determining whether a statement is scientific or not, falsification does not suffer from the same issue.

(Continued)

The statement 'all swans are white' can clearly (and easily) be falsified – you simply need to find a swan that is not white. Once that idea has been falsified you must then abandon it or modify the idea to accommodate the new observation of the non-white swan. The statement could easily be modified to 'most swans are white' for example. Falsification is a far better way, concluded Popper, of determining and demarcating science from non-science or pseudoscience. The principle of falsification is something that can (and should) be applied to all ideas as a means of determining whether or not it is scientific.

Deductive reasoning is, at its simplest, theory confirming. It is based on deductive logic, which starts with a set of premises or axioms (true statements) and proceeds towards a logical conclusion. For example, here is a classic yet simple example of deductive logic:

First Premise (axiom) – all men are mortal.

Second Premise (axiom) – Socrates is a man.

Conclusion – Socrates is mortal.

The conclusion of the argument, that Socrates is mortal, is in logical terminology both sound and valid. An argument is sound if its premises are true. Conclusions are valid when the premises are true, and it is impossible for the conclusion to be false.

Deductive arguments may also be invalid. This happens when the premises are true, but the conclusion is false, or does not logically follow on from the premises, for example:

First Premise – Mary is an honest woman.

Second Premise – Mary is a politician.

Conclusion – all politicians are honest.

In this instance, while both premises may be true, so it is a sound argument, the conclusion does not logically follow on, and therefore the argument is invalid.

Inductive reasoning

A key characteristic of a conclusion based on inductive reasoning (see Figure 5.3) is that it is more probable rather than certain. In this respect, while the conclusions from deductive reasoning are generally certain, i.e. when the premises are true, the logical conclusion may also be viewed as 'true', in inductive reasoning the conclusions are more likely to be true than not. Inductive reasoning moves from the specific (the observations and data) to the general, i.e. theories. It is a form of theory building rather than theory confirming.

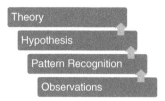

Figure 5.3   Inductive reasoning – this begins with observations and builds towards theory

Inductive reasoning is useful when the data you have are limited. For example, if you have completed questionnaires from a sample of a population, you cannot claim that you have the answers from the whole population. Depending on the type of sample, you may be able to generalise that because your sample shows 'X' it is probable that 'X' is the case. You will not be able to say that 'X' is true in all instances. There are methods of sampling that can be considered as representative of the whole population, but these have always been treated with a degree of scepticism, e.g. in the case of political polls.

Biology is a good example of a discipline where induction is used. Biologists tend to gather data (observations) from nature and from there build to a theory. In evolution, for example, observations of the anatomical, physiological and biochemical similarities between different species, along with fossils of pre-existing but now extinct organisms, lead to the theory of evolution by natural selection. The observations, which can include DNA analysis, of the similarities between species are explained by the theory.

Abductive reasoning

As noted earlier, this form of reasoning is described commonly as 'inference to the best explanation'. In many ways it is similar to inductive reasoning, i.e. it is based more on probability than on certainty. It is a form of reasoning that takes general observations or data and then proceeds to devise the simplest, yet best explanation for the observations/data available at that point in time. Abductive reasoning can be said to be pragmatic. It may not give the 'true' conclusion or even the most probable conclusion, but an abductive conclusion will be good enough to be useful when applied in real life. Within the philosophy of science, scientific realism utilises an abductive approach.

Qualitative and quantitative approaches in education research

Qualitative and quantitative approaches to research are differentiated by the use of words and numbers:

- Qualitative research generally uses words, narratives, observations and descriptions.
- Quantitative research converts or gathers data in the form of numbers that can be subsequently manipulated, often using statistical techniques.

These basic descriptions of the two approaches hold true in a general sense, but it would not be accurate to say qualitative focuses 'only' on words or that quantitative utilises 'only' numbers. As Yilmaz (2013, p.311) defines it, quantitative research 'explains phenomena according to numerical data which are analysed by means of mathematically based methods, especially statistics'.

Numerical data may not always be gathered through measurement and instruments. For example, a researcher could count the number of times a teacher mentions a specific keyword in a lesson, or count the number of times a child puts up a hand to answer a question in a day. Both of these activities will generate numerical data that may form part of a quantitative analysis for research purposes.

Qualitative research is defined in various ways, with no one definition serving all the various disciplines that utilise qualitative methods and methodologies. One of the most comprehensive definitions comes from Denzin and Lincoln (2011, p.3):

> Qualitative research is a situated activity that locates the observer in the world. It consists of a set of interpretive, material practices that makes the world visible. These practices transform the world. They turn the world into a series of representations, including field notes, interviews, conversations, photographs, recordings, and memos to the self. At this level, qualitative research involves an interpretive, naturalistic approach to the world. This means that qualitative researchers study things in their natural settings, attempting to make sense of, or to interpret, phenomena in terms of the meanings people bring to them.

As you can see, it is very different from the quantitative approach to research favoured by the natural sciences. This does not mean that qualitative methods cannot result in numbers that could be analysed using quantitative methods, but generally qualitative approaches are very much more interpretive.

Comparing qualitative and quantitative research

Qualitative research is described as 'naturalistic' (Flick, 2009), i.e. it records situations as they happen in the real world. While the researcher is often a part of the situation they are researching, this does not mean that they will overtly change or seek to influence events as they happen – they are bystanders who observe and record what happens as it happens. One aspect of qualitative research is that there is no expectation about what findings will emerge and therefore no constraint on the actual findings. Overall, this is an inductive approach where patterns, hypotheses and theories emerge from the data, rather than being a deductive approach that seeks to determine whether a predicted result is supported by the data.

Table 5.1 sets out the key differences between a quantitative and qualitative approach to research.

Table 5.1 Qualitative versus quantitative approaches to research (sourced from Anderson, 2010, Babbie, 2013, Morgan, 2013, Yilmaz, 2013)

	Quantitative	**Qualitative**
Assumptions	• An objective reality exists • The researcher and the 'researched' are independent • Variables can be identified • Observations/measurements can be made that result in numerical data • Research is axiologically value free and objective	• Reality/realities is/are socially constructed • The researcher is not independent of the object(s)/subject(s) being researched • Variables are difficult to identify due to their complex nature • Data gathered are mostly in a narrative form but not exclusively non-numerical • Research is axiologically value bound and subjective
Purpose	• To confirm hypotheses or predictions often derived from theory • To quantify variation • To describe the characteristics of a population • To predict and/or establish causal relationships	• To develop theories (grounded theory) and then hypotheses • To describe and interpret variation(s) • To describe the characteristics of a defined sample of a population • To predict possible future behaviour • To describe group 'norms'
Approaches	• Key questions are derived from existing theory (in deductive approaches) • Mostly experimental • Requires large datasets to ensure validity • Data collection is focused on measurements or coding of data into numbers • Statistical analysis	• Questions are designed to generate data • Data 'emerge' from various observations, interviews or documents • Data collection is focused on collected narratives, free responses (e.g. questionnaires) or researcher accounts of observed situations • Interpretive analysis

(Continued)

Table 5.1 (Continued)

	Quantitative	Qualitative
Summary of the key characteristics	• Data are usually gathered with highly structured instruments • Large sample sizes representative of the population being studied • Reliability is achieved through replication or protocols that can be repeated by other researchers • There is a clearly defined research question (or questions) • Data are reported in number form and as statistical results accompanied by tables, charts, figures etc. • Research results may be used to generalise ideas more widely, predict future results or reveal causal relationships (through deductive reasoning)	• Provides a realistic view of the 'lived world' that cannot be shown numerically • Researcher gains insight through immersion and direct interaction in a culture or situation • Researcher can describe existing phenomena and current situations • Has flexible and multiple ways of data collection, analysis and interpretation • Has the ability to promote new ways of understanding people, society and complex social situations • Can be responsive to changes in conditions and situations (e.g. needs of participants) and allows flexibility to refocus research when necessary • Provides a holistic view of the situation/subjects under study • Allows for identification of patterns in descriptive primary and unstructured data • Can lead to the development of testable hypotheses that, if confirmed, may develop into new theory (through inductive reasoning)

Qualitative research

Qualitative research is purposeful in that it often consists of case studies of people, events, incidents etc. as the researcher believes that it will yield 'rich' data, i.e. data that are meaningful, from which understanding will emerge. It is not a prime consideration of qualitative research that the emergent understanding is necessarily generalisable. In order to best gather meaningful data, qualitative research designs are often adaptive, so that if/when situations change they can be responsive.

Data collection

Various methods of data collection are used in qualitative research (see below) with the aim of accumulating 'rich data' (as noted above). Often, this comes in the form of direct quotations from individuals and/or group interviews. These capture individual perspectives and form what is called a 'lived experience'. Such data have their own issues (e.g. Are people's memories fallible or infallible? Will the accounts of two different people about a single incident ever be exactly the same?), but ultimately personal perspectives are, unlike a lot of quantitative data, context rich. As the ultimate goal of qualitative research is not the production of primarily generalised and widely applicable outcomes, such issues are not problematic but must be recognised. It should also be recognised that in qualitative research the researcher is not always detached from what is being researched. In social sciences there are two terms that cover the position of the researcher and the viewpoints that they have of the subject being researched, i.e. *etic* and *emic*. If a researcher is within the social group or part of the research, this is described as an emic position. Etic means that there is a level of detachment and separation from what is being studied.

Data analysis

As noted earlier, a lot of qualitative research is inductive in nature. Observations are made, data are gathered, and the first job in analysis is to begin to recognise patterns within the data. This is often done by identifying themes and inter-relationships within and between datasets. This is a form of inductive analysis that uses inductive reasoning to come to conclusions about what the data show.

Qualitative research also engages a holistic perspective, i.e. the whole phenomenon under study is considered, not just a part. It is also recognised that what is being studied is a complex system that will have multiple variables and possibly numerous interdependencies. In the process of analysing data it is important to realise that complex systems may not easily be simplified, and that it is all too easy to mistake associations for correlations and then to apply a cause and effect solution (see Box 5.3).

BOX 5.3 IS EXCESSIVE SCREEN TIME HARMFUL TO CHILDREN?

In 1988 research was published that described how children and young people's (CYP) increasing 'screen time' (i.e. watching television) was leading to the displacement of other, more healthy activities. This so-called displacement theory concluded that viewing TV for more than four hours per day resulted in 'effects [that] were negative and increasingly deleterious' (Neuman, 1988 p.414). This research guided a lot of policy with respect to advice to parents on monitoring and limiting children and young people's screen time. It suggested that the harmful effects of technology were directly proportional to the time spent engaging

(Continued)

---

with that technology. There was a direct claim here of cause and effect. Since 1988 the options for increasing screen time have multiplied due to the advent of smartphones, tablets and laptop computers.

Digital screens are now a fixed feature of day-to-day living, and they can appear in many devices that in 1988 would not have been envisaged, e.g. touch screen satellite navigation, ticket purchasing machines, in-store shopping and stock checking, even checkouts in supermarkets. A recent systematic review of research on children and young people's screen time and mental health concluded that 'the evidence indicated that moderate use of digital technology is not intrinsically harmful and may be advantageous in a connected world' (Przybylski and Weinstein, 2017 p.204). A 'systematic review of reviews' (Stiglic and Viner, 2019 p.1) of the effects of screen time on the health and well-being of children and young people concluded that:

> There is evidence that higher levels of screentime [sic] is associated with a variety of health harms for CYP, with evidence strongest for adiposity, unhealthy diet, depressive symptoms and quality of life. Evidence to guide policy on safe CYP screentime [sic] exposure is limited.

On reading this conclusion you could imagine that the reaction to the review would be to suggest that the earlier work of Neuman is correct, but the keyword here is 'associated'. There is no *direct* correlation that would lead to higher levels of screen time causing obesity etc. Overall, what the research shows is that there is no hard evidence that increased screen time will have a negative causal effect on children and young people's overall health and well-being. Moderate use, it was found, could lead to a marginal increase in well-being. The 2017 research, which was specifically designed to test for any links between well-being and screen time, tested a proposed 'Goldilocks theory', i.e. that there is a point where screen time is 'just right' and can lead to a moderate increase in well-being (Przybylski and Weinstein, 2017).

Human beings are complex

Reading various research papers and reviews on screen time and its effect on CYP and their well-being, one thing is clear. There is no simple rule, no guidance that is unambiguous and fully evidenced on what is the 'right' amount of screen time. As most authors admit, the variables to take into consideration are multiple and also complex. Internet-connected devices can be educational, and if misused they *may* be harmful. How children interact with each other socially is also complex. We may like to think that in-person contact is best in real life. That said, person-to-person contact across the internet can also be positive (e.g. you can easily link in real time, face to face, with a 'pen pal' in another country), whereas in the pre-digital age such interactions by letter were slow and far less dynamic. Such long-distance interactions could have a very positive effect in educating young people about different cultures and environments.

In most studies such as these, the outcomes could be categorised as 'common sense'. What one family decides is acceptable for them may not suit the lifestyle of others. As the authors of the latest studies state, we should worry less about screen time, but ensure that, overall, we put in place commonsense rules that safeguard things like sleep, physical activity and the appropriate use of websites/apps. Where there are known issues, such as the blue light emissions from screens that disrupt and limit melatonin production, thereby affecting the ability to fall asleep naturally, imposing limitations, such as no screen time one hour before bedtime, may be very sensible.

Quantitative research

The data and datasets for quantitative research will almost exclusively be in the form of numerical data. The purpose of such research is often about testing and confirming existing hypotheses/theories, and it is predicated on being able to generalise from the specific. The output from quantitative research is often more strictly formulaic than qualitative research. There are expectations for good quantitative research that certain criteria are met.

Protocols for quantitative research reporting

When researchers report their results, they tend to follow a protocol to ensure that important features of their data are accurately conveyed and shown.

The first element reported is a description of the data gathered. The type of data collected is described, i.e. whether the data are nominal, interval or ordinal etc. At this point, there will be an outline of what general statistical procedures will be applied to the data. The analysis and interpretation of the data are left until later. The next element is to alert the reader to any incomplete or anomalous data and to whether the data differ from what was expected to be gathered – this is normally described in the methodology and methods section of the research.

If inferential statistics are used, then the confidence intervals should be stated, the degrees of freedom and at what level of significance the data is being reported at (e.g. $p = 0.05$). At this point it is useful to state whether there appears to be any correlation/causation. Remember, however, that correlation does not automatically lead to causation, and this is the case particularly if the research is non-randomised. It is useful to check that any statement implying causation is logical and has other evidence to support the link. For example, there is a correlation between skill in mathematics and shoe size. As a shoe size increases, so too does skill in mathematical understanding – it is almost directly proportional. Foot growth, of course, does not cause greater mathematical skill, as there is an underlying cause (the child is getting older and their exposure to formal education and teaching in mathematics increases).

Some of the strengths of quantitative research are that it involves large numbers of subjects, that population samples can be representative, and that it can generate large amounts of data which improve the accuracy of findings. These features help to make quantitative research more valid and reliable. With the addition of things such as randomised controlled trials, it can also help to make findings more generalisable and secure.

Being able to reproduce and replicate quantitative studies is also viewed as an inbuilt safeguard for reliability and validity. As quantitative studies usually mean applying statistical tests to large datasets, there is less chance of the researcher introducing a personal bias. A criticism of this is that such techniques lack context.

A common claim for the results of quantitative research is statistical significance. Reporting that the outcome of research is statistically significant adds great weight to any argument or claim. Statistical significance is often presented as a number, known as a 'p-value', where p = probability. P-values, however, are not without problems and some statisticians urge caution when using and relying on these (see Box 5.4).

BOX 5.4 STATISTICAL SIGNIFICANCE

Statistical significance testing is based on three things: hypothesis testing, a normal distribution (often called 'the bell curve'), and a p-value. Statistical significance looks at how likely it is that the relationship between two (or more) variables is caused by something other than chance.

How a golfer hits a hole-in-one could be explained by various factors (or variables), e.g. distance to the hole, experience and ability of the golfer, familiarity with the hole, type of club used, weather conditions etc. However, for most non-professional golfers there is an additional, large element of chance. For professional golfers, chance still features as a significant factor in making a hole-in-one. If a non-professional golfer during a normal round of golf on a full-size course hit two or more holes-in-one consecutively, then statistically we might say that this is most likely not due to chance. As far as can be ascertained, no professional golfer has scored two holes-in-one at consecutive holes in the same round of golf. Only three professional golfers have scored two holes-in-one at non-consecutive holes in the same round of golf during a PGA tour. Which brings us to a report of what is the most unlikely ever round of golf played by an amateur.

The former leader of North Korea, Kim Jong-il, was once reported to have played a round of golf that resulted in a 38 under par round. This included no fewer than 11 holes in one (Anon, 2011). Statistically this is 'improbable' in the extreme. The most likely explanation is that people stationed on the course deliberately placed the leader's wayward shots close to or in the hole.

Normal distributions

A normal distribution is a distribution of what you would expect to find, naturally, when measuring various things. For example, people's feet show a normal distribution. There are some (a few) people with very small feet, and some (a few) with very large feet. Most people have feet that cluster around the average size. A normal distribution is sometimes called a bell curve due to the shape of the graph that results when you plot measurements that occur naturally (see Figure 5.4):

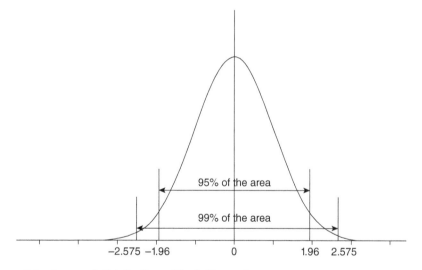

Figure 5.4   A normal distribution – 'the bell curve'

(Source: http://methods.sagepub.com/book/interpreting-quantitative-data-with-ibm-spss-statistics-second-edition/i650. xml?fromsearch=true)

Source details:

Chapter Six | Normal distributions and sampling distributions. In: *Interpreting Quantitative Data with IBM SPSS Statistics* by: Rachad Antonius. Published: 2013 (2nd edn). DOI: http://dx.doi.org/10.4135/9781526435439.n6

(Continued)

Many things, from body measurements to test scores, or salaries in companies, often conform to a normal distribution. It is therefore a very useful way of looking at research data. It is likely that most of what we want to measure and investigate will conform to a normal distribution. There are some key things about a normal distribution that are worth bearing in mind.

The measurements of central tendency, the mean, median and mode, are all the same in a normal distribution. The curve of the graph is normally a symmetrical one with the line of symmetry centred on the mean. This means 50% of the measurements plotted fall to the left of the mean (below average) and 50% to the right of the mean (above average). As you move away from the mean, you begin to measure how much a value deviates from the mean figure – what is called a 'standard deviation'. A standard deviation is a measurement of how spread out your data are. The smaller it is, the closer to the mean the data are, the taller the peak on the normal distribution is (a taller 'bell') and the smaller the tails are. The bigger it is, the further away from the mean your data are and this results in a smaller peak (a flatter 'bell').

The 'empirical rule' in statistics determines the percentage of data that fall within a certain number of standard deviations from the mean. In a normal distribution, 68% of the data are within one standard deviation, 95% of the data are within two standard deviations and 99.7% of the data are within three standard deviations of the mean. Overall, the area under the curve in a normal distribution is '1', i.e. it represents 100% of the population under study.

Hypothesis testing

In quantitative research you are testing hypotheses to see whether your idea is correct or not. There are set rules and methods used for dealing with numeric data and performing statistical tests. The process begins with the development of a hypothesis. In statistics, the hypothesis you present as the one you are trying to show is incorrect is known as the null hypothesis. The null hypothesis is that statistically there is no difference between variables. For example, if we were testing whether boys or girls are better at riding a bike, the null hypothesis is that there is no difference between boys and girls when it comes to riding a bike. Having formed this hypothesis you then formulate what is called the 'alternative hypothesis', i.e. what you think the outcome is most likely to be if the null hypothesis is not proven. In this instance, your alternative hypothesis would be that either boys or girls are better at riding a bike.

Let's imagine you decide to do some research to explain how well children perform in tests at different times of the day. Having looked at some online research (Dimitriou, 2015, Williams, 2017), you think that there is evidence that suggests children do not perform well first thing in the morning. Your finding from reading the research is that it shows that teenagers find it difficult to get up in the morning, so delaying the start of the school day and examinations is a good idea and they may get better grades as a result.

The null hypothesis in this example would be that 'there is no difference in children's performance in tests related to the time of day the test starts'. The alternative hypothesis is the one that states there is a statistically significant relationship between two variables, so your alternative hypothesis here would be that given two variables (morning and afternoon), 'Children perform better in tests that are timed to start in either the afternoon or first thing in the morning'.

You would then gather data (test outcomes/scores for a chosen sample of children) from tests that were timed to start in the morning and in the afternoon, ideally from the same or a matched sample of children. There would have to be some serious thought given to generating the sample so that it was representative. You would need to think about the age of the children, and the tests that they were doing (e.g. are they equivalent in levels of difficulty, subject level, type of test etc.?). You would then perform relevant statistical tests to see whether there was indeed a difference in outcomes. Reporting on these tests will involve stating the level of significance you were testing at and the outcomes in terms of any p-value.

What is a p-value and why is it problematic?

A p-value is a number between 0 and 1. It is a measure of statistical significance, but it can be misused and misunderstood. The p-value relates to the null hypothesis. A small p-value, i.e. $p = 0.05$, would indicate that the null hypothesis should be rejected. What this is often interpreted as meaning in practice is that you are saying there is only a small possibility that the alternative hypothesis you are testing for is false, that 95% of the time it's more probable that your alternative hypothesis is correct. The problem with this is that a small p-value does not mean that the hypothesis is proven, or that it is correct or true, it simply means that the null hypothesis is rejected. In this example, a small p-value would mean we reject the idea that there is no difference in children's test results related to the time of day.

The problem with p-values boils down to whether or not an observed effect is real or could be the result of random chance. The use of p-values is designed to try and rule out this randomness. Often the cutoff point for p-values is $p = 0.05$. Some studies will boast that they tested with a p-value of 0.01 – i.e. 1% rather than 5%. In both cases however, calculating a p-value is actually concentrating on the wrong thing – the null hypothesis. What ideally we would like to do is prove that the alternative hypothesis is true, and a p-value just does not do that.

Common methods of data collection in social science research

The methods used to gather data for social science research are many and varied. Some of the more common ones are described below with an outline of their characteristics, strengths and weaknesses.

Surveys

Surveys can generally be divided into two types, questionnaires and interviews. Both involve asking questions of people and recording the answers given, manually or electronically. Technically, a 'survey' could be anything from a quick handwritten question-and-answer form to a very intensive in-depth set of questions conducted and recorded electronically as a verbal interview. The survey method chosen should be suitable for the scale and overall purpose of the research project.

Questionnaires

With the advent of the internet and e-mail, questionnaires are now much easier to construct and distribute widely. In some instances pen-and-paper questionnaires could be used, especially if you are dealing with people who do not have access to computers and the internet, or where the population being studied may not be able to use computer-based questionnaires. Surveys utilising mobile technology are now frequent, and people are more used to being texted to provide some form of feedback, e.g. if they have interacted with customer services for a particular product or service. This can have a negative effect, as many people find such automated surveys intrusive and annoying. That said, there is often (or should always be) an opt-out mechanism to allow people to ignore such requests. There are many similarities between questionnaires and interviews, e.g. both can utilise open and closed questions, both can elicit short- or long - form answers to questions, and both can generate 'rich' data.

There are many different types of questionnaires and the data that are gathered can be qualitative as well as quantitative. In dealing with the results of questionnaires, qualitative data can also be coded to produce quantitative data. The commonest forms of questions are shown in Table 5.2; it is not an exhaustive list but it does cover the main types of questions used.

Advantages of using questionnaires

Questionnaires are very flexible and can be very cost-effective. With the advent of the internet their cost has been much reduced from the days when postal questionnaires

Table 5.2 Questionnaire and question types

Questionnaire Type	Question Types
1. *Structured Questionnaires*: Often, but not exclusively, used in quantitative research. These are sometimes referred to as 'closed' questionnaires. Responses are limited and pre-coded to generate number values.	• Matrix questions: The question is followed by one or more rows of possible responses which can be checked/ticked by respondents. These are essentially multiple choice questions in the format of a grid. • Contingency questions: These questions appear only when respondents provide a specific type of answer to a previous question, i.e. the question presented is contingent upon the previous answer.
2. *Unstructured Questionnaires*: These are more often used in qualitative research. As the name implies, they do not have set structures and the questions will be open-ended. This means the respondent is free to provide as little or as much information as they want, and to specify, in regard to the question, what is most important to them.	• Simple, general, 'open' questions that ask for a response to matters such as beliefs, family circumstances, current affairs etc.
3. *Scaled Questionnaires*: These are also useful for quantitative research and ask respondents to provide answers by selecting a specific rating.	• Leading questions: These questions force a response to a particular scale. The scale is designed such that all possible answers are equally as likely given a normal population; they are leading in that the scale defines and 'leads' the person to only consider the response in set terms, e.g. bad or very bad, good or very good etc. • Likert questions: These questions use various scales in order to ascertain the level of agreement a respondent has with specific statements. Likert scales usually vary from 3-7 possible responses. Many Likert scales use either 5 or 7 response categories. • Dichotomous questions: These have a simple one or other response type structure, e.g. yes/no; true/false. • Bipolar questions: These require respondents to choose between two given extremes. • Importance questions: These require respondents to choose a specific rating on a scale (e.g. 1–5) with defined extremes.

were the main method of reaching large numbers of people. Questionnaires ensure that the same questions are asked of all participants. It is also possible to control who gets the questionnaire, so you can define your sample group, and with pre-qualifying questions online you can control for key characteristics whether your survey is generally available, i.e. you can ask key questions to determine whether the person trying to respond would be suitable, and part of the demographic you are trying to survey.

The responses to questions can be controlled and pre-defined, and the results can be statistically analysed, as much of the data can be numerical or coded to generate numerical data. Open narrative responses can be captured, and these may also be analysed by software designed to deal with qualitative data, e.g. NVIVO.

Questionnaires allow respondents time to reflect and answer or you may have timed answers if you wish. In terms of reproducibility and replicability, questionnaires can be shared and used by others who wish to carry out similar research or verify outcomes with other similar samples of respondents from elsewhere (e.g. another country, region etc.). Large numbers of responses will generate lots of data and this can help improve accuracy.

Anonymity can also be useful if a researcher wishes to gather more 'honest' responses. It is easier to guarantee anonymity with an online questionnaire than it is with a face-to-face interview, and this can help to reduce bias.

Disadvantages of using questionnaires

Although questionnaires are very common, there are some key disadvantages in using them as a research and data-gathering tool:

- The quality of the data is dependent on the quality of the questions being asked. If questions are poorly worded, introduce a bias or are unclear, then the data derived from this will also be poor or may be inherently biased.
- Questionnaires can be viewed as impersonal and many people do not like to engage with them. There is the possibility of getting small numbers of respondents or people who start an online questionnaire but do not complete it. This latter point is a danger with long questionnaires. A poor response rate is one of the major disadvantages of questionnaires.
- Some respondents will not take online surveys seriously and may respond in ways that are unpredictable, e.g. in rating-type questions they always provide the same rating regardless of the question. In open questions there is no way to know whether the responses provided are true.
- Questionnaires with open-ended questions could generate a lot of data that will take a long time to analyse and code. With open-ended questions, the researcher is unable to clarify meaning or ask the respondent to elaborate on an answer. If the questionnaire is anonymous then there can be no follow-up. This is also an issue if the respondent does not understand the question, as there is no interaction with the question setter who may be able to provide clarification.

Interviews

Interviews are arguably more powerful than questionnaires in gathering data for qualitative research. They will, however, be much more work intensive and take more researcher time than questionnaires, as each interview will require researcher time to conduct the interview.

Fundamentally there are three main types of interview carried out for research purposes:

1. Structured.
2. Semi-structured.
3. Unstructured.

How these are carried out will vary, as will the length of interview and the conditions under which the interviews are conducted.

1. *Structured interviews*

   These interviews are rather rigid in that the interviewer is required to follow a set procedure and ask a set series of questions. This is the closest an interview comes to being a questionnaire. There are no prompts from the interviewer once the set question is asked and there is no elaboration of the question. Follow-up questions are either absent or built into the script used by the researcher. Structured interviews do not necessarily allow for depth, as the lack of follow-up questions and the limited interaction between the researcher and interviewed person do not allow for depth. Structured interviews can have the advantage of being quick to administer (depending on the overall number of questions) and they can be administered by a range of people who may not necessarily have an in-depth understanding of the research.

2. *Semi-structured interviews*

   As the name implies, semi-structured interviews will have a series of 'set' questions, but they do allow for follow-up questions related to the main question. They also have the advantage of allowing a good researcher to probe more deeply interesting responses or comments made by the person being interviewed, and if necessary elaborate on the meaning of the question if the interviewee is unsure what the question means. The person conducting this type of interview necessarily would need an understanding of the subject and field of research in order to most effectively carry out a good interview.

3. *Unstructured interviews*

   These interviews are claimed by some (Corbin and Morse, 2003; Ritchie et al., 2013; Jong and Jung, 2015) to deliver the most in-depth accounts from people. An unstructured interview has been described as more of a purposeful conversation than an interview (Yeo et al., 2014). The fact that unstructured interviews have little planned in advance does not mean that they are serendipitous or easier than structured or semi-structured interviews. They may appear to be chaotic, but an experienced researcher will have selected participants carefully and formed a bond with them so that the conversations are not just random, but will have some meaning and, as noted above, purpose. While this type of interview may result in the most meaningful data, they are more difficult to conduct and time-consuming.

A major advantage in conducting face-to-face interviews is the ability to gather contextual data. How a person answers questions, their hesitations, gestures, facial gestures etc. can all add to the richness of the interview data.

Observation

Observation of participants in social science research has been used in a variety of settings. In education it may be the observations of teachers and teaching, children as learners, or it could be the observation of both in different situations, e.g. in early years 'play', the school as a place of social interactions, children within and outside classrooms. What is common for all observations is that the researcher will undertake some form of systematic description of the events being observed. Observations may be made in person by researchers or research assistants, or they could be remote (live by video feed or recorded). Lewis-Beck et al. (2004, p.752) define observation as 'a data collection strategy involving the systematic collection and examination of verbal and nonverbal behaviors [sic] as they occur in a variety of contexts'. A specific advantage is that observation should take place in a natural setting in which those being observed behave naturally – that said, the act of being observed can, in itself, make people uncomfortable and they may not act naturally, and thus it's greatest perceived strength can also become its greatest weakness. Setting up the right conditions for observation is paramount to the success of the process. When done well, observations can 'facilitate understanding of what people do and how these can alter in response to situations and over time, especially where people find their own practice difficult to articulate' (Walshe et al., 2012 p.1048).

Summary

One chapter cannot do full justice to the range and type of methods used by social science and education researchers. There are many textbooks that will tell novice and experienced researchers how to perform research, and these will provide detail on the various strengths and weaknesses of different methods. The purpose of this chapter was to provide a general understanding of the two main approaches to research – qualitative and quantitative – and how these align with experimental and interpretive methods.

Central to any research is how the researcher comes to reasoned conclusions based on the data gathered. In this respect, understanding deductive, inductive and abductive reasoning is critical. When you read and interpret research, understanding how the researcher has used data to draw their conclusions will enable you to seek out illogical conclusions or confirm that the conclusions are indeed sound and valid.

The various methods used by researchers will often involve surveys, in the form of questionnaires or interviews, and understanding how these may be constructed will enable you to more easily judge the validity of the approach taken, and the quality of the questions asked. In this respect it is worth remembering the different forms that bias can take, as outlined in Chapter 3.

In the next chapter we will examine how research is written and the various structures that research takes when it is presented in different publications.

Further reading

Ritchie, J., Lewis, J., Nicholls, C.M., & Ormston, R. (2013) *Qualitative Research Practice: A Guide for Social Science Students and Researchers* London: Sage

This is a comprehensive textbook written by a team of leading researchers associated with NatCen Social Research (the National Centre for Social Research). It covers the entire process of qualitative research from beginning to end – moving through design, sampling, data collection, analysis and reporting.

Thomas, G. (2016) *How To Do Your Case Study* London: Sage

Thomas, G. (2017) *How to Do Your Research Project: A Guide for Students* London: Sage

The two titles above are popular and well-written books that are very accessible to undergraduate and postgraduate students. These are not textbooks, as such, but explain in plain language how to carry out a case study or how to design and carry out a research project.

Bibliography

Anderson, C. (2010) Presenting and evaluating qualitative research *American Journal of Pharmaceutical Education* Vol.74 No.8 p.141

Anon. (2011) 50 fascinating facts: Kim Jong-il and North Korea *Telegraph*, December 19th

Babbie, E.R. (2013) *The Basics of Social Research* Boston, MA:Cengage Learning

Corbin, J., & Morse, J.M. (2003) The unstructured interactive interview: issues of reciprocity and risks when dealing with sensitive topics *Qualitative Inquiry* Vol.9 No.3 pp.335–354

Denzin, N.K., & Lincoln, Y.S. (2011) *The SAGE Handbook of Qualitative Research* Thousand Oaks, CA: Sage

Dimitriou, D. (2015) Why children who sleep more get better grades [online]. The Conversation (UK). Available at: http://theconversation.com/why-children-who-sleep-more-get-better-grades-51828

Flick, U. (2009) *An Introduction to Qualitative Research* London: Sage

Jong, Y.O., & Jung, C.K. (2015) The development of interview techniques in language studies: facilitating the researchers' views on interactive encounters *English Language Teaching* Vol.8 No.7 p.30

Lewis-Beck, M.S., Bryman, A., & Futing Liao, T. (eds) (2004) Types of observation. In *The SAGE Encyclopedia of Social Science Research Methods* Thousand Oaks, CA: Sage pp.752–757

Morgan, D.L. (2013) *Integrating Qualitative and Quantitative Methods: A Pragmatic Approach* London: Sage

Neuman, S.B. (1988) The displacement effect: assessing the relation between television viewing and reading performance *Reading Research Quarterly* Vol.23 pp.414–440

Przybylski, A.K., & Weinstein, N. (2017) A large-scale test of the Goldilocks hypothesis: quantifying the relations between digital-screen use and the mental well-being of adolescents *Psychological Science* Vol.28 No.2 pp.204–215

Ritchie, J., Lewis, J., Nicholls, C.M., & Ormston, R. (2013) *Qualitative Research Practice: A Guide for Social Science Students and Researchers* London: Sage

Stiglic, N., & Viner, R.M. (2019) Effects of screentime on the health and well-being of children and adolescents: a systematic review of reviews *BMJ Open* Vol.9 No.1 e023191

Walshe, C., Ewing, G., & Griffiths, J. (2012) Using observation as a data collection method to help understand patient and professional roles and actions in palliative care settings *Palliative Medicine* Vol.26 No.8 pp.1048–1054

Williams, J. (2017) Why both teens and teachers could benefit from later school start times [online]. The Conversation (UK). Available at: http://theconversation.com/why-both-teens-and-teachers-could-benefit-from-later-school-start-times-72525 [accessed January 9th 2019]

Yeo, A., Legard, R., Keegan, J., et al. (2014) In-depth interviews. In Ritchie, J., Lewis, J., McNaughton-Nicholls, C., & Ormston, R. (eds) *Qualitative Research Practice: A Guide for Social Science Students and Researchers* (2nd edn) London: Sage, pp. 178–210

Yilmaz, K. (2013) Comparison of quantitative and qualitative research traditions: epistemological, theoretical, and methodological differences *European Journal of Education* Vol.48 No.2 pp.311–325

6

How Research is Written

Chapter aims

- Understand the function of research reporting
- Be aware of the structure of research report writing
- Understand the characteristics of different forms of research reporting

Introduction

There are many genres in writing, from fiction to biography, even textbooks. Each genre will have certain characteristics. Common advice given by experienced writers to novice writers is to read as many different examples as possible of the genre they wish to write within to understand the characteristics and how such books or articles are structured. Similar advice is also valuable for anyone wanting to understand research. Read different examples of research to appreciate how they are structured and understand the key characteristics of good research.

In this chapter, some common forms of research report are outlined and deconstructed to help you begin the process of understanding the genre. The chapter begins by looking at the functions that research report writing serves and explains two common approaches – idiographic and nomothetic – to reporting social science research. After that, a common structure for research reporting is described. The bulk of the chapter details the characteristics of different forms of research outcomes such as case studies, ethnographic studies, meta-studies etc.

The more familiar you are with research, and the purposes, structure and functions of different types of research, the easier it will be to understand and critique these. This chapter sets out the basic requirements of the more common forms of social science and education research reporting, but there are many different ways to write about research and not all of them can be covered in a single book chapter.

The functions of academic report writing

Education research is about people, as is social science in general. Predominantly, academics write about children or young people when they consider education research, though there is a large body of work on adult and higher education. Children do not exist independently of the adults and others with whom they mix and live. This adds to the complexity of research.

The aim of any research is to provide explanations. Ideally, research should uncover new explanations for existing phenomena. One problem with how we view the world, and how we see and understand social interactions, is that we try to rely on past experiences to explain new and/or novel situations. There is a danger of fitting evidence to a known or desired explanation, thereby introducing bias.

Idiographic and nomothetic approaches

In social science two terms are commonly used in describing the approach to gaining knowledge from research, i.e. an idiographic or a nomothetic approach. The essence of these approaches is the difference between being specific and generalising. An idiographic approach is typical in social science research. It is about individuals and their unique characteristics. It assumes, rightly, that no two people are the same, act the same, have the same life history or experience things in the same way. The nomothetic approach is more common in scientific research. It is about generalising and delivering explanations in the form of theories and descriptions of events (laws) that can be applied generally. In nomothetic descriptions researchers tend to categorise events or sort them into various typologies.

The purpose of research reports

In writing up research reports, academics and others will seek to do three things, i.e. describe, explain and persuade. They may not do these things in equal measure in all research reports, but overall, we can think of the function of academic report writing as consisting of these three things. Figure 6.1 sets out a continuum along which research reports can be placed. Box 6.1 sets out the key characteristics of descriptive, theoretical and persuasive reports.

Functions of Academic Report Writing

Observational/Descriptive	Theoretical/Explanatory	Persuasive/Influential
Documents the observations made, describes 'what is' in a neutral way with no central thesis or theory. It is a factual representation of a situation. Reports may also be historical and describe what has happened, not just what is happening.	These reports will offer an explanation or theory as to how or why something has happened. They may also apply existing theory to new situations. There are sometimes relationships described in a cause and effect way.	Reports that are aimed at influencing policy or persuading people of a particular course of action. Reports will have interpretations and evaluations of the observations. There is a clear development of an argument and the report will make recommendations or outline a particular position (ideological/political etc.). Such reports are aimed at people with influence.

Figure 6.1   The functions of academic report writing

BOX 6.1 KEY CHARACTERISTICS OF DESCRIPTIVE, THEORETICAL AND PERSUASIVE REPORTS

Descriptive/observational reports

The function of this type of report is not to provide answers, but to merely document situations. Such reports will describe observations made by researchers.

(Continued)

They are, and should be, value free and simply document 'what is'. These reports may also document historical situations and contexts through descriptions of archive documents, films, audio etc.

Theoretical/explanatory reports

A theory is an evidenced and generally accepted explanation of something (e.g. a natural phenomenon in science). Often, either research reports will use an established theory in which to explain the observations/data gathered, or the observations/data will lead to the construction of a new theory (explanation). This is often referred to as 'grounded theory'. The theory is constructed 'from the ground up' to provide an explanation; it is an inductive approach. The purpose of 'theory' is to explain how or why something happens. Where possible, the cause of an effect should be explained by theory, but a complication here is the issue of confusing correlation with causation (see p.99–100).

Persuasive/influential reports

In research terms 'impact' is important. When research is being conducted and reported, the notion of impact will be thought about carefully. Who is the research aimed at? How will it be received? How widely can it be distributed and how can it influence practice and policy? All these things are part of the impact agenda. For research to have impact it must have a clearly developed argument with relevant and logical interpretations and evaluations of the observations/data gathered. Research that has impact will have a set of recommendations which can be implemented by others, such as school management teams, politicians etc.

For any report to have value it must inform. The structure of reports will vary, but generally they will follow a pattern that provides an introduction, a summary of the findings (often called an 'executive summary'), and recommendations. These serve to allow the reader to quickly grasp the most important aspects of any report – what the author found out and what they think this means. In research papers published in journals this often takes the form of an abstract; it sums up in a couple of hundred words at most what the paper is about and what it found out.

The main body of a report will also vary in structure, but it must set out the problem or area being investigated and why it is important. It should summarise what is already known, with reference to prior work, and the approach being taken in the study. This will be followed by the methodology and methods used. Any potential limitations that could affect the interpretation of the data can be set out within this section. The results section sets out the collected data (quantitative and/or qualitative) in a logical and coherent form. The discussion is the place to talk about what the results mean and how they evidence any outcomes. The conclusion draws all the key aspects of the report together, and may suggest further research that could be undertaken or implications for policy and/or procedures.

For social science studies, experiments are not a common method of investigation. The outcomes of social science research are therefore much more varied than a traditional scientific approach which relies heavily, and sometimes exclusively, on experimental methodologies.

Common ways of publishing and writing about social science research include formats such as case studies, ethnographic studies and phenomenographic studies. Many researchers also take a mixed methods approach, so their reports may well include experimental and quantitative outputs as well as wholly qualitative reporting. Table 6.1 sets out some of the key reporting formats for social science and educational research.

As we saw in Chapter 1, published research can take many forms and the hierarchy of publication means that different forms will have different characteristics. Generally, we can think of research outputs as academic, professional or general. Crudely these three forms of research output will have increasingly complex, subject-specific forms of language that will relate directly to the audience at which the publication is aimed.

The structure of research reports

Most research reports/articles follow a standard set of headings. In some cases, research journals will have a recommended layout for research papers that authors must follow, particularly when it comes to the reference style used. The way in which research evidence is presented and explained across the social sciences is very similar. There is a commonly used organisational framework for presenting research, as follows:

1. *Introduction* – this defines the problem being researched, usually in the form of a research question and the rationale for the research as well as summarising the outcomes.
2. *Literature review* – in this section what is currently known (or where there are gaps in knowledge) relating to the problem or subject of the research is set out.
3. *Methodology and methods* – this section anchors the research in a paradigm and sets out the methods used to gather the data/evidence.
4. *Results or findings* – for quantitative methods this may be in the form of tables, graphs or charts. In qualitative research it may consist of narrative descriptions of observations or extracts/transcripts from interviews etc.
5. *Discussion* – Here the author will delve into the meaning of the findings and link these to specific sources in the literature review. The key question that needs to be answered is 'What do the findings mean?' rather than simply restating the findings from the previous section.

6. *Conclusion* – this normally begins by restating the answer(s) to the initial research question(s), based on the findings. This section also provides space to make recommendations for further research or changes to policy/practice.
7. *Reference list or bibliography* – the sources used, particularly within the literature review, will be listed according to the reference style required by the journal/publisher.
8. *Appendices* (if needed) – these may include raw data, descriptions of survey instruments, longer extracts from interviews etc.

Many, if not all of these sections can be found in the various forms of research reports discussed below. Table 6.1 outlines the characteristics of a variety of research reports. What follows is a more detailed description of some of the more common research outputs in social science and education.

Table 6.1 Characteristics of academic reports

Group	Type	Characteristics
Reports	Technical	• Have a clear and straightforward writing style that informs the reader about the subject matter and relays information in a clear and concise manner. • Use direct language and often incorporate technical or specific language that professional/experts will understand but which may not be understood by the general public. • Will be structured, detailed and informative. • Do not normally address problems or questions.
	General	• Should have a clear, logical structure. • Are selective and designed to convey meaning in a general way. The selection of words is critical to ensure that meaning is conveyed correctly, and technical or specific terms should be defined and/or explained. • Objectivity is an aim, so issues are examined from more than one viewpoint. • Should be factually accurate and contain verified information. • Should be clear enough to answer the questions in the minds of readers.
Studies	Case	• Provide a holistic view of a social phenomenon. They are written to try and provide understanding of complex situations. • The 'case' will have boundaries that define it. • Are selective and do not aim to generalise about any particular actions or phenomena. • Aim for depth rather than breadth when describing the detail of the 'case'. • Use multiple sources of data.

Group	Type	Characteristics
	Ethnographic	<ul><li>Examine people's social interactions in their natural environment (work, home, during leisure etc.)</li><li>Aim to provide an in-depth account of people's views and actions and any interactions they may have, e.g. with technology.</li><li>Aim to understand how people view the world.</li><li>Are detailed accounts of people's lives and interactions.</li></ul>
	Longitudinal	<ul><li>Take place over long periods. They are observational in nature and often result in large datasets that cover many thousands of participants.</li><li>Some are national, e.g. the Millennium cohort study that has 19,000 participants studying child development, social stratification and families in the United Kingdom.</li><li>Depending on access to data, they may be retrospective, i.e. they can examine existing data (e.g. medical records), or prospective, i.e. specifying new data to be gathered over time.</li><li>Require repeated observations of the same people over time.</li></ul>
	Phenomenographic	<ul><li>Look at and interpret the different ways people experience or think about things.</li><li>Are descriptive and focus on the various perceptions people have of their experiences.</li><li>Focus on the various ways people experience things and how these are described or observed by the researcher.</li></ul>
Reviews	Systematic review	<ul><li>A specialised form of literature review that aims to use systematic methods to collect, review and critically analyse the findings of a body of published research.</li><li>Are intended to provide a complete summary of 'the current state' of research on a particular question or concept/idea.</li><li>Are often used in healthcare as a way of compiling the best evidence related to treatments, trials etc.</li></ul>
	Meta-analysis	<ul><li>Is similar to a systematic review but uses statistical analytical methods to combine the results of previously published results of quantitative studies.</li><li>Will have a methodology that explains what previous research has been included or excluded and why.</li><li>Statistical methods will be explained and will show how the results deal with error.</li></ul>
Experimental	Randomised control trial (RCT)	<ul><li>Aim is to try to eliminate bias</li><li>Are considered to be the 'gold standard' for clinical research and trails.</li><li>Purpose is to try and test the effectiveness of a particular treatment, drug or approach. In education, this could be related to pedagogical approaches.</li><li>Key aspects are the idea of randomisation and the use of a 'control' group.</li><li>Another issue is the ability to control variables so that the target and control group outcomes can be fairly compared.</li></ul>

(Continued)

Table 6.1   (Continued)

Group	Type	Characteristics
	Action research	• It is often determined by the researcher(s) as a problem or issue that needs to be solved in a particular context and often at the time the research is undertaken. • Can be completed by individuals or small groups with a view to understanding a situation or improving an approach/situation. • Normally an iterative process.
	Experimental	• Usually reserved for scientific studies, especially in clinical/medical trials or in experimental psychology. • Experiments are designed to try and predict the outcome of a situation by looking at and controlling various independent and dependent variables. Three key features of experimental design are reliability, validity and replicability.

Case studies

Strictly speaking, a case study is a research design that will include within it various methods such as interviews, questionnaires, observations, document analyses etc. As Tight (2017 p.6) says:

> The term 'case study' is, or should be, reserved for a particular design of research. Where the focus is on in-depth study of one or a limited number of cases. In practice, however, its use is rather messier and more complex.

As Thomas (2016 p.9) puts it, 'it is a focus and the focus is on one thing, looked at in depth and from many angles'. Case studies will involve the study of social phenomena (Swanborn, 2010), and providing an agreed single definition of exactly what a case study is can be difficult. Those who utilise case studies within their research will present their own view of what a case study is. Two 'big hitters' in the game of case study research are Robert Stake and Robert Yin; their work has been very influential and most researchers will look at their seminal textbooks on the subject (Stake, 1995; Yin, 2013).

One of the main benefits of using case studies is the ability to look in depth at something. It is also an extremely flexible approach to research which can encompass many qualitative and quantitative methods. One of the main limitations of case study approaches is the lack of generalisability. This is, however, a contentious issue in that not all researchers agree on this point (see below).

Validity and reliability in case study research

Thomas (2016 p.64) asks an interesting question when it comes to issues of validity and reliability in relation to case studies: 'Do I have to worry about validity and reliability in a case study?' His answer is a simplistic and categorical 'no'. He admits that this is not a universal response to the question and that others will question his simple dismissal. His response is interesting. He notes that issues of reliability and validity have been imported from other research paradigms (he mentions applied psychology). He also asserts that in such disciplines, instruments used to measure certain features do, in practice, need to be reliable and have a degree of validity, i.e. the idea is that the same instrument (e.g. a questionnaire) should be able to elicit similar outcomes in different study populations. Thomas (2016 pp.64–67) argues that a case study is very particular and only examines a particular 'thing' at a 'particular time' by a 'particular researcher'. There is nothing to say that the same 'thing', if investigated by another researcher at a different point, would result in similar or the same outcomes.

Simons (2009 p.128) does, in part, concur with Thomas. She is not as categorical, but warns that in attempting to ensure the reliability and validity of your data, by meeting criteria not meant for social sciences, there is a danger of 'straining the data to meet the concept and losing the meaning in the process'.

A general concern, noted by Swanborn (2010), is that case studies cannot lead to generalisations. This view is contested by others. Yin (2013), for example, takes an interesting stance by thinking about what we mean by 'generalisation'. He considers two types – statistical generalisation, and what he terms 'analytic generalisation', the latter being generalisations that inform theoretical concepts used in the design of the case study, or that result in new concepts that arise from the case study on completion. Simons (2009 p.164) has a view, which is that case studies are not about producing generalisable results, but are more about how we can 'demonstrate how and in what ways our findings may be transferred to other contexts or (be) used by others'.

Ethnographic study

Defining precisely what ethnographic research is (and is not) is no simple matter. As Hammersley (2016 p.1) says:

> ... there is often disagreement about what count and do not count as examples of [ethnography]. Furthermore, the meaning of the term overlaps with that of several others – such as 'qualitative method', 'interpretative research', 'case study', 'participant observation', 'life history method', and so on.

The essence of ethnography is the study of people's behaviour in everyday contexts; it is as close as you can get to real life as is possible. Data are gathered not by experiment, or in a laboratory, or in artificial surroundings, but from the direct observations of the researcher. Rather than structured or semi-structured interviews, interaction with the people being 'studied' takes the form of informal everyday conversations. There is, at the outset, no detailed plan for how data are gathered or indeed what data are to be gathered. The data (which may include video and audio, but more commonly are in the form of detailed field notes written by the researcher) are true 'raw data'. Unlike case studies, where there are necessarily distinct boundaries, a characteristic of ethnographic studies is the absence of pre-determined boundaries.

The focus for ethnographic research is often confined to a relatively small group of people, perhaps connected by the setting or location in which they find themselves. Where the focus is a single person, it is often referred to as 'life history' research.

Once data have been gathered, interpretation is often iterative, i.e. it is subject to analysis and re-analysis in a circular way until meaning and understanding are apparent. There are usually no pre-set categories for analysis and no pre-determined outcomes/predictions. If any statistical methods are used, they tend to be simple quantitative ones such as measurements of word frequencies etc. These support the analysis and are not the focus of that analysis.

Phenomenographic study

Phenomenography is an interpretivist qualitative methodology. The aim of phenomeno-graphic studies is to understand how people interpret the world, how they experience things and in what ways they interact with 'things' (e.g. technology, objects etc.).

The central idea of phenomenology is subjectivist, i.e. it assumes the world exists but that people will experience it in different ways. They will, in effect, construct their own reality, and different people will construct it in different ways.

Like ethnography, phenomenography is very descriptive. The interviews conducted to gather data about different people's understanding of the world, and their experiences of it, will be more structured than an 'informal conversation' (as described above).

The analysis of data is also an iterative process and seeks to place the various descriptions given by people into 'categories of description' (Marton and Pong, 2005). Researchers look for the variance between descriptions to understand the different viewpoints from which those being studied perceive the material world. This is sometimes referred to as the 'theory of variation' (Pang, 2003).

Take care not to confuse phenomenography with phenomenology. The latter is very different – it is more philosophical and aims to study things such as consciousness, human emotions, human judgement etc. It deals in aspects of human experience and thinking that are not necessarily tangible in a materialistic sense.

Systematic reviews and meta-analyses

A useful form of research publication in social science and education research is a systematic review. This form of research takes a well-defined research question and then collects and summarises as much of the 'known' research as possible.

Systematic reviews are highly structured reports which have well thought-out methodologies and methods that will clearly state what research is included, and more importantly, why any research is excluded. The research will have set inclusion and exclusion criteria that are applied to the various searches undertaken. The aim of such a review will be to use pre-defined and comprehensive search terms (see Chapter 2) and then read carefully the titles, abstracts and keywords so that unsuitable studies can be eliminated. High-quality systematic reviews will involve two or more researchers who will screen the papers, and where possible researchers will contact experts within the field to ensure that all major and important studies are included.

Once the shortlist (which may include many papers) has been compiled, the studies are then critically appraised. The purpose of a systematic review is to provide a summary of all the empirical evidence available for the concept, idea or process being reviewed. The best can be an invaluable indicator of the current state of play in relation to a research field. Box 6.2 describes one such systematic review that looked at the issue of learning styles in education.

BOX 6.2 LEARNING STYLES

Learning styles have been used (or more accurately misused) in schools for several years. The idea that children (people) learn 'better' in their preferred 'learning style' – often stated as being visual, auditory or kinaesthetic – has been an urban myth circulating between teachers, business managers and education consultants (and a few initial teacher educators). This zombie pedagogy refuses to die, despite lots of evidence against the central idea that preferred learning styles make a difference. In 2004 a major systematic review was conducted to critically analyse the research evidence on learning styles. What follows is a summary of that systematic review.

Learning styles and pedagogy in post-16 learning: A systematic and critical review

Overview of the report

The systematic review was carried out by a team of researchers from the UCL Institute of Education, the University of Newcastle and the University of Exeter (Coffield et al., 2004). The review was commissioned by the Learning and Skills Research Centre and supported by the then Department for Education and Skills (now the DfE).

The report itself was set out in nine sections and was 182 pages long. The aim of the review was to answer four key research questions:

(Continued)

1. What models of learning styles are influential and potentially influential?
2. What empirical evidence is there to support the claims made for these models?
3. What are the broad implications for pedagogy of these models?
4. What empirical evidence is there that models of learning styles have an impact on students' learning? (Coffield et al., 2004 p.3)

In addition to these questions the review aimed also to:

- identify the range of models that are available, influential or potentially influential in research and practice;
- locate these models within identifiable 'families' of ideas about learning styles;
- evaluate the theories, claims and applications of these models, with a particular focus on evaluating the authors' claims for reliability and validity;
- evaluate the claims made for the pedagogical implications of the selected models of learning styles;
- identify what gaps there are in current knowledge and what future research is needed in this area;
- make recommendations and draw conclusions about the research field as a whole. (Coffield et al., 2004 p.3)

The review had very clear questions and aims. In all, the authors 'identified 71 models of learning styles and . . . categorised 13 of these as major models' (Coffield et al., 2004 p.1).

The review identified 3,800 papers and reports initially as potential candidates for inclusion in the review. Having drafted and applied selection criteria, this was whittled down to 838 texts that were reviewed and placed in their database. This was further reduced to 631 texts, which are listed in the final report. As you can see, it was a major task. To help with their inclusion/exclusion process the researchers looked at things such as whether or not the text had been widely quoted or cited, whether the 'learning styles' they mention were based on any explicit theory, how representative the texts were of the literature as a whole, and whether or not the text led to further research by others or whether any surveys or inventories used were widely used by teachers or others.

The main sections of the report then critically reviewed and analysed many of the more common 'learning styles/inventories' to judge whether or not they were indeed effective. The report looked in detail, for example, at Honey and Mumford's Learning Styles Questionnaire, Kolb's Learning Style Inventory and the Myer's Briggs Type Indicator. Their overall conclusion was as follows:

Learning style researchers do not speak with one voice; there is wide-spread disagreement about the advice that should be offered to teachers, tutors or managers. For instance, should the style of teaching be conso-nant with the style of learning or not? At present, there is no definitive answer to that question, because – and this brings us to the second problem – there is a dearth of rigorously controlled experiments and of longitudinal studies to test the claims of the main advocates. (Coffield et al., 2004 p.140)

A meta-analysis is similar to a systematic review in that it gathers together current empirical evidence, but in addition to reviewing the methods and reliability of research done, it also combines the data from various studies to provide a summary of all the results obtained by research using further statistical analysis. In the world of medicine, systematic reviews and meta-analyses are helpfully collected together by the Cochrane Collaboration. This is an online database of systematic reviews on healthcare interventions including drug trials, randomised controlled trials (see below) and other reviews. It allows healthcare professionals to quickly and comprehensively see 'what works' and whether certain procedures would be suitable for their patients. In education, the Education Endowment Foundation (EEF), established in 2011, was set up by the Sutton Trust with funding from the Department for Education (DfE). This provides a similar service, on a much smaller scale, to teachers and educationists. The EEF fund and make accessible research, systematic reviews and meta-analysis pertinent to education.

A major meta-analysis of educational interventions was published by Hattie (2009, 2011). In his books Hattie synthesises over 800 meta-analyses of educational interventions and ascribes to them an 'effect size'. This generates a visual and numeric indication of how much of an effect any particular intervention will have on a child's attainment. Hattie is widely cited and reviewed. Some researchers have criticised his approach, including how he calculates his effect sizes (Bergeron and Rivard, 2017; Rømer, 2019). His work has, nonetheless, provided a substantial body of analysis of educational interventions.

Randomised controlled trials (RCTs)

Randomised controlled trials are seen by many as the 'gold standard' in research. For medical research it is imperative that any new procedure is subjected to an RCT before it is widely put into use. Any intervention, be it medical or educational, will carry potential risks and benefits. It is easy to argue that the risk in medical terms is more acute than in the educational domain – after all, a poor intervention or an un-researched intervention could easily result in death or a permanent disability. In education it is very unlikely that the outcomes will be as extreme, but the widespread use of an intervention that has no benefit or may prove detrimental can have a significant effect on the learning and educational progress of children.

In an ideal world, all educational interventions should be subject to rigorous testing, research and – where possible – randomised controlled trials, so that if and when the intervention is made more widely available, teachers and others will have confidence that the intervention will do no harm educationally.

A problem in education is the spread of interventions that superficially may seem to have a positive effect, but when looked at more closely have no substantial empirical evidence to back up the assertion that an effect is real and/or positive. Learning styles and Brain Gym were two interventions that appeared to have an effect, but when looked at more closely and examined critically and scientifically had no discernible effect. Both these interventions spread through the education community, often through word of mouth or via educational consultants who specifically 'sold' the ideas to schools during professional development sessions (Buch, 2014). One explanation for an apparent positive change being seen is the Hawthorne effect (see p.80). Any change or intervention, especially if the group or person delivering the intervention is aware that they are being monitored, may well result in an effect regardless of the intervention being made.

For RCTs there are some specific conditions that need to be met (Hutchison and Styles, 2010):

- The intervention must be aimed at a specific population of individuals.
- Any 'improvement' must be measurable and linked to the educational attainment of the individuals taking part in the intervention.
- When the intervention is evaluated there must be a discernible 'effect' which can be described.

The benefits of RCTS in education are that it may be possible to generate a causal conclusion from an intervention (either positive or negative) or that the outcome is neutral (it has no effect). RCTs will also eliminate selection bias as children are allocated randomly rather than manually to an intervention or control group.

Objections to RCTs have come from a range of people. Some will state that withholding an intervention that may be beneficial to children is unethical – especially for the control group, which purposively does not receive the intervention. In medical trials this is overcome by using a practice known as 'blinding', where either the patient and/or the practitioner is unaware that the 'intervention' is being carried out. For a drug trial this is relatively simple: a placebo (i.e. a drug/pill that has no active ingredient) can be provided. Where neither the patient nor the medical practitioner knows whether the treatment is a placebo, this is called a 'double-blind' trial. In education this is much more difficult to achieve since interventions – especially changes to pedagogy – will be clearly visible and known to the teacher and children. A counter to this is that if an intervention is genuinely new and innovative, you cannot know that the outcome will be positive. In this instance, ethically you are not knowingly depriving a group of a potential benefit. If you are sure the intervention will be beneficial, then there is no need for an RCT, but you will need to question how you know this, and what the evidence is that shows any intervention to be beneficial.

Other objections to RCTs in education include the idea that human interactions and group interactions (children with other children, parents and children, teachers and children etc.) are so complex, that designing a simple procedure that can 'control' for all the variables is almost impossible. Even if two teachers are using the same intervention, how they enact that intervention will differ simply because they are different personalities, different teachers.

A constant issue in education is the implementation of new interventions, procedures, practices, and even curriculums/specifications. Politicians often invoke the mantra that a child's education is too important for new ideas and interventions to wait, that a child only has 'one chance'. Wholesale reform is a constant issue for teachers and has been for many years. The problem is that RCTs can and do take time. Having sufficient robust evidence in place before major change is implemented is not politically expedient. Governments are often only in place for one or two terms of office (five to ten years), and those in control of education – e.g. in England, the Secretary of State for Education – much less (on average two to three years at most).

From May 2010 to August 2019 there have been five different politicians in post as Secretary of State for Education. The longest tenure during that period was served by Michael Gove, who was in post from 11 May 2010 to 15 July 2014. The shortest tenure lasted from 8 January 2019 to 24 July 2019, just 198 days. To make a political mark with voters, there is intense pressure to introduce widespread, untested, new procedures and interventions, with insufficient robust research to attest to any demonstrable effect.

Summary

Academic writing is a genre that has many ways of being executed. One common characteristic is the need for reference to and citation of research to back up any claims being made. Descriptive prose and narrative are not uncommon, but they are used judiciously to illustrate observations or aid explanations. While many academic reports will follow a traditional format, as set out earlier, there is a great deal of variety in how research is presented in the social sciences and in education.

When you read academic research, doing some background reading about the researcher (when possible) is always a good move. It is worth finding out something about the research paradigm the researcher works within and reviewing other research they may have published. This will help you understand how they are presenting their evidence and what assumptions they may have made.

Understanding what type of report you are reading, what it is intended to accomplish (to deliver theory, persuade etc.), is also important. Carrying out any form of critical analysis (see Chapter 7) requires you to understand what the author intended to present.

Further reading

Hammersley, M. (2016) *Reading Ethnographic Research* Abingdon: Routledge

Ethnographic research takes time to understand. This guide sets out how to identify the key arguments in an ethnographic study and how to assess such studies.

Stake, R.E. (1995) *The Art of Case Study Research* London: Sage

This is one of the standard texts on case study research, written by one of the foremost experts. It is a comprehensive guide to doing case study research.

Thomas, G. (2016) *How To Do Your Case Study* (2nd edn) London: Sage

As with Gary Thomas's other books, this is an easy-to-read and accessible text on how to carry out case study research.

Yin, R.K. (2013) *Case Study Research: Design and Methods* (Applied Social Research Methods) Thousand Oaks, CA: Sage

Along with Stake, Yin's book is the other key text on how to carry out a case study. Yin and Stake differ in approach and detail, but between the two authors you have what amount to the 'definitive' works on case study research.

Bibliography

Bergeron, P.-J., & Rivard, L. (2017) How to engage in pseudoscience with real data: a criticism of John Hattie's arguments in visible learning from the perspective of a statistician *McGill Journal of Education/Revue des sciences de l'éducation de McGill* Vol.52 No.1 pp.237–246

Buch, P. (2014) Neuromyths and why they persist in the classroom [online]. Sense About Science. Available at: http://archive.senseaboutscience.org/blog.php/77/neuromyths-and-why-they-persist-in-the-classroom.html (accessed May 22nd 2017)

Coffield, F., Moseley, D., Hall, E., & Ecclestone, K. (2004) *Learning Styles and Pedagogy in Post-16 Learning: A Systematic and Critical Review* London: Learning and Skills Research Centre

Hammersley, M. (2016) *Reading Ethnographic Research* Abingdon: Routledge

Hattie, J. (2009) *Visible Learning: A Synthesis of Over 800 Meta-analyses Relating to Achievement* Abingdon: Routledge

Hattie, J. (2011) *Visible Learning for Teachers & Students: How to Maximise School Achievement* Abingdon: Routledge

Hutchison, D., & Styles, B. (2010) *A Guide to Running Randomised Controlled Trials for Educational Researchers* Slough: NFER

Marton, F., & Pong, W.Y. (2005) On the unit of description in phenomenography *Higher Education Research & Development* Vol.24 No.4 pp.335–348

Pang, M.F. (2003) Two faces of variation: on continuity in the phenomenographic movement *Scandinavian Journal of Educational Research* Vol.47 No.2 pp.145–156

Rømer, T.A. (2019) A critique of John Hattie's theory of visible learning *Educational Philosophy and Theory* Vol.51 No.6 pp.587–598

Simons, H. (2009) *Case Study Research in Practice* London: Sage

Stake, R.E. (1995) *The Art of Case Study Research* London: Sage

Swanborn, P. (2010) *Case Study Research: What, Why and How?* London: Sage

Thomas, G. (2016) *How To Do Your Case Study* (2nd edn) London: Sage

Tight, M. (2017) *Understanding Case Study Research* London: Sage

Yin, R.K. (2013) *Case Study Research: Design and Methods* (Applied Social Research Methods) Thousand Oaks, CA: Sage

PART 3

APPRECIATING AND UNDERSTANDING RESEARCH

7
Understanding Criticality

Chapter aims

- Define what is meant by criticality
- Examine different ways of being 'critical'
- Understand different forms of criticality
- Identify common flaws in arguments
- Be aware of common logical fallacies

Introduction

It is very common to receive feedback on academic work that includes phrases such as 'this work would be improved with a more critical approach to the literature' or 'you need greater criticality'. Understanding what this means requires a student to understand what the word 'critical'/'criticality' means within the context of research. This chapter explores the concept of criticality and examines what criticality 'is' and 'is not'.

Criticality can be viewed as the evaluation of arguments presented within research. It encompasses deciding whether the materials being cited are appropriate and recent, or if they are not recent, whether their importance as a piece of work makes them seminal or influential. When you weigh up the evidence for and against an argument, you are utilising criticality. The outcome of a critical analysis process will allow you to assess whether the author of a piece of work has proven their point and come to logical conclusions from the evidence presented. It should alert you when an author is displaying any form of bias (see Chapter 3 for a more detailed discussion on forms of bias).

The chapter begins with a definition of criticality. It then looks at ways of being 'critical' and explores some examples of poor critical thinking and flawed arguments. Finally, it explores fallacies in argumentation – these are things to avoid when critically analysing any research, as they distract from the actual arguments and divert attention away from the core ideas being put forward.

Defining criticality

There are several related and sometimes synonymous terms that fall into the 'critical' stable: critical thinking, critical engagement, critical analysis, critical reading and critical writing. They will have crossover elements, such as looking for justified reasons for a conclusion or solution, or evaluation of evidence.

A good way of looking at the idea of being critical is to look at the complete opposite. What does it mean to be uncritical? Generally, it would mean simply accepting what you've read or been told is true, not bothering to ask about the evidence to support a claim. As Chatfield (2017 p.3) suggests, it is when 'we take things at face value without pausing to consider whether this is sensible or justified'.

A key requirement of criticality is objectivity. When you approach something objectively, you are taking a neutral stance. This requires you to ensure you are not unduly influenced by either one person or one 'take' on an issue. You also need to be sceptical, not just of anything you read but of your own views on an issue as well. Developing a neutral approach takes practice. Unfortunately, no matter how much you strive to be neutral and objective, or even to be a good sceptic, you will never be 100% successful. It is just part and parcel of being human that we will have weaknesses that will affect our neutrality and objectivity, and the sooner we recognise this the better. It does not make criticality redundant or impossible, it simply means that we must be on our guard and try our best to ensure we keep those inherent biases at bay.

Having established what criticality is not, we must now try to define what it is. Criticality is the ability to use information and apply questioning and logic to ascertain the veracity of the information provided. Criticality allows us to locate information within a broad context and see links between the particular (what we are reading about) and the general (the broader context). Finally, criticality allows us to discover the weaknesses and the strengths in the arguments we are looking at. Criticality is a cognitive process; it is about how we think. It also utilises aspects of philosophy – what influences how we think.

Critical thinking and critical engagement

Critical thinking, sometimes referred to as critical engagement, draws on two academic disciplines: philosophy and cognitive psychology. Together they provide a foundation for critical thinking and the skills necessary to carry it out successfully. It is very common in job specifications to have phrases like 'the ability to think critically' or 'the post requires a good critical thinker'. As indicated at the start of this chapter, feedback on academic writing often implies that a greater degree of critical thinking is necessary in order to obtain high marks. Understanding how philosophy and cognitive psychology combine reveals the key skills necessary for critical thinking.

Critical thinking and philosophy

Our view of reality, of the world as it is, is shaped by our experiences. This means it also shapes how we think. To be a good critical thinker we need to move beyond our reality and consider that there may be other realities. While at first this sounds as if we are going into some sort of 'wacky' philosophical discussion about whether or not there is a reality or that there are multiple realities, the idea is not as strange as you may think. To help us, we need to think about how Plato wrote about the effect of education on an individual, and how a lack of education changes who we are and how we think (see Box 7.1).

BOX 7.1 PLATO'S CAVE

In Plato's famous book *Republic*, he describes a conversation between his brother, Glaucon, and his mentor, Socrates. Socrates proposes a situation where a group of people are chained in a cave in such a way that they can only see the blank wall in front of them. Behind them is a fire. Objects – between

(Continued)

the chained-up people and the fire, including the people themselves – cast shadows on the wall of the cave. For these prisoners the shadows represent reality. They can see nothing except the shadows and how the shadows move as the flames flicker or the objects move or are moved. They cannot move their heads or bodies and see what is to the side or behind them. If this is their experienced reality and it is all they know, then they have no need or want to try and break free or escape. They are comfortable existing in their reality.

Socrates then describes what may happen if one of the people chained up is freed. They would be able to turn around and see the objects that create the shadows (the only form of reality the prisoner has known). If they were then told that what they are now seeing is reality, not the shadows on the wall, the likelihood is that the person would reject that explanation and insist that the shadows were reality. They may insist that the objects were not real or were not the source of the shadow reality. The released prisoner would be likely to want to return to facing the wall, as that is what is comfortable and known and returns the prisoner to a state of ease rather than the stress of being faced with a new, unknown and very different reality.

Socrates continues: what if the prisoner is then taken from the cave, past the fire into the daylight? At first things would be so new and so painful to look at, the prisoner's natural reaction would be to close their eyes and remember the reality of the cave (imagine emerging into strong sunlight after a long period of complete darkness). Once their eyes had adjusted to the daylight, the prisoner may well see things that are reminders of the shadows in the cave, such as reflections and new shadows. They may also see that objects are the source of the shadows, with the sun (which is analogous to the fire in the cave) being the source of the light. The prisoner may then redefine reality to take on board the new information and the new facts discovered, and reality would be changed for them.

For Socrates, a philosopher is like the freed prisoner who begins to realise that there may be a different reality – a different way of seeing things and understanding their situation/circumstances.

The lesson for critical thinking is for people not to be imprisoned within their own constructed reality, but to be open to see the possibilities of other realities and to be flexible enough to change their thinking.

Critical thinking requires people to suspend their personal realities and contemplate the idea that there may be other realities, that there could well be explanations for things other than the most obvious or common explanations.

Critical thinking and cognitive psychology

Cognitive psychology is the study of how we think. Cognitive psychologists try to produce models of how we process information. They look at things such as memory, perception and what it means to be conscious (i.e. our awareness of being rather than simply the state that is the opposite of unconscious).

Cognitive psychology contributes to our understanding of critical thinking by adding in our ability to be reflective and evaluative. These are skills that allow us to reflect on how we think. They allow us to analyse our thoughts and see potential flaws or strengths in our thinking. In other words, these are analytical skills.

Critical analysis

A tendency that is easily identified in student writing is being descriptive rather than analytical. An analysis of any piece of writing or research must move beyond the descriptive. University work and research necessarily move beyond what we know, what we can easily and simply describe, into areas that are new or unknown. This will involve reformulating what we know into new and novel explanations of the facts. The outcome of good critical analysis is the construction of a strong argument that is backed by evidence. Critical analysis will also allow us to refute counterarguments or show that existing arguments are less than convincing, less well supported by the evidence, or wrong. The use of critical analysis is not confined to academic essays or even to research. We use the skills associated with critical analysis every day, even when we are discussing what could be considered as everyday events (see Box 7.2).

BOX 7.2 THE FORWARD PASS

Football and rugby are huge sports that attract millions of supporters. In the days before high-definition television (HDTV) and ultra-high-definition TV (UHDTV) technology, third match officials and now the video-assisted referee (VAR), there were many arguments up and down the country about whether or not someone was offside when they scored a goal or try. When discussing the pros and cons of a refereeing decision people use (often unconsciously) critical analysis. They use evidence, usually based on their view of the match and their knowledge of the rules, from either the vantage point of being in the crowd or watching it on television. They construct their argument that the goal or try was either good or should have been disallowed. The arguments with family, a friend, or colleagues would usually come in the form of arguments and counterarguments about what

(Continued)

had been seen. Each person will construct their 'reality' based on the evidence they have to hand. Some people will rank the evidence using criteria they believe will strengthen their position. Someone who had attended the match may claim their attendance means they saw what happened as it happened in real life. They could claim that viewing something on a television, years ago, was not good evidence, with a fuzzy picture or in black and white. Counterarguments may relate to the fact that in real life the incident could have happened at a distance from where the spectator was standing. It could be argued that on television the camera can zoom in on the action, even in a limited way, and there may well be replays.

In modern times, real-life observation could be seen to be less significant evidence than a picture relayed by modern HD or UHD technology to a remote location where it could also be instantly viewed from different angles. Ultimately, the decision rests with the referee who is, arguably, closer to the action than any camera, and who is immersed within the game and able to react to the situation as a trained professional, not just a spectator with a bit of knowledge. Referees are trained professionals who know, understand and have passed tests and examinations on how the rules of the game should be applied in various circumstances. Even so, many spectators and amateur experts will still disagree with some decisions. In a lot of cases this is the result of an inherent bias, i.e. being a passionate supporter of a team. Less often a mistake is made.

The essence of critical analysis is used by people every day, and in many different situations. Certain conditions must exist for critical analysis to work effectively. If these conditions are not fulfilled, then critical analysis will not be possible. For example, there is no point in me trying to contribute to an argument about who wrote Shakespeare's plays. I am neither an expert on the life and work of Shakespeare, nor am I sufficiently knowledgeable to be able to analyse writing styles forensically to determine the authorship of any classical work. On the other hand, I may be able to argue more effectively claims that I see being made about the problems relating to fracking, earthquakes and contaminated water supplies, as my background of studying geology has provided me with some expert knowledge.

Knowing, understanding, evaluating, applying, analysing and synthesising

Critical analysis requires certain conditions to be met (the process of critical analysis will be set out in more detail in Chapter 8). These are as follows:

- *Knowing*: the ability to recall previously learned information, usually from our long-term memory rather than our short-term memory.
- *Understanding*: the ability to compare, organise, translate and interpret ideas and knowledge, often in new and novel situations. It involves the use of facts that derive from knowledge.
- *Evaluating*: the ability to apply judgement to opinions and arguments to assess their veracity and validity.
- *Applying*: the ability to use knowledge and understanding to solve problems in (usually) new situations which often require the use of previously acquired rules and techniques in new or different ways.
- *Analysing*: the ability to break down large amounts of information or reduce complex information into more easily digestible parts. This leads to being able to make inferences about the information or to ascertain the author's motives.
- *Synthesising*: the ability to combine or compile information in new and different ways, leading to new or alternative solutions to problems or the presentation of the synthesised information in new and different patterns.

These conditions are often referred to as 'higher order thinking skills', but this phrase is problematic in some ways as it implies that they are hierarchical and that one cannot be achieved without first achieving the level below. This is most famously associated with one of Bloom's taxonomies, i.e. the cognitive domain.

Bloom's cognitive domain

Benjamin Bloom was an educational psychologist. In the 1950s he headed a committee that devised a series of taxonomies of learning. In 1956 the first taxonomy, the cognitive domain (based on knowledge), was published, with two other taxonomies – the affective domain (based on emotion) and the psychomotor domain (based on actions) – produced later. The purpose of developing the domains was to improve the relationship between the curriculum, its assessment, and teachers' understanding of learning.

The cognitive domain was set out as a stepped pyramid with the base of the pyramid being knowledge. As you climb the pyramid, you pass through the following levels: comprehension, application, analysis, synthesis, and – the pinnacle of the pyramid – evaluation.

In the 1990s one of Bloom's students, along with others, made changes and revisions to the original pyramids. For the cognitive domain the new order started with remembering at the base, followed by understanding, applying, analysing, evaluation, and finally a new 'pinnacle' – creating.

Too often when Bloom's was/is taught and used, people saw/see it as a hierarchy. Knowledge becomes a 'lower order' skill, i.e. just 'knowing things'. The goal was always seen as achieving the highest level, i.e. 'evaluation' in the original domain. The problem resides in thinking of the pyramid as hierarchical in nature.

The newer revised synthesis of Bloom changes the 'top' level to creating. This revised taxonomy suffers from the same issue in that it is presented as a pyramid and therefore potentially as a hierarchy. Rather than conceive these skills as hierarchical, it is better to envisage them on a plane where they have equal status and then consider the links between them. If any of these skills is foundational and essential for any form of thinking, it must be knowledge/remembering (i.e. recall of knowledge). Without knowledge we have nothing to work from. Understanding comes from knowledge, as does application (of knowledge), synthesis (of knowledge), analysis (of the knowledge), evaluation (of the knowledge) and creativity.

Bloom's taxonomy and knowledge: a new synthesis

What it means to 'know' something or to 'understand' is riven with contradictions and misconceptions. Some philosophers of science equate knowledge and understanding (Achinstein, 1983; Lipton, 2003; Grimm, 2006), while others see knowledge as different from understanding (Kvanvig, 2003; Pritchard, 2014; Zagzebski, 2017). Those who equate knowledge and understanding often conceive of understanding as the accumulation of knowledge, i.e. the more knowledge you have the more understanding you have. Philosophers of science, who would follow such a view, have a general consensus that understanding is a 'species' of knowledge. The idea is that knowledge does not just come in one form (see Table 7.1). A key question is whether you can have understanding without knowledge and vice versa. Some philosophers (e.g. Pritchard, 2014) argue that understanding without knowledge is possible, and certainly having knowledge of something does not always lead to understanding. We must also think about how understanding differs from knowledge, if we believe it to be different. Knowledge does not come in degrees, i.e. you either 'know' a fact or you do not. You cannot have a degree of knowledge about a fact. For example, Queen Victoria was born on 24 May 1819 – making three facts: the day, the month, the year. You may know one, two or all three of these facts, or have no knowledge at all about when she was born. There is no 'degree' of knowledge here. Even if you say 'I think she was born in the 1800s as that's when the Victorian era was', your knowledge is incomplete. You will 'know' that Victoria defines the Victorian era and that (most, some, all?) of that era was in the 19th century. You will have two facts but whether you fully understand what the Victorian era was all about is very debatable. Learning all the facts of when the Victorian era began and when it ended would still not necessarily provide a full understanding of the Victorian era. It is possible, however, to understand what the Victorian era was about, and how it is characterised in history, but still not actually know how it is defined datewise.

Understanding does come in degrees. You can have a little understanding of what causes matter to have mass, a lot of understanding, or no understanding at all. There is a continuum along which your understanding would move from zero (the position of the majority of people who have not studied quantum physics) to a very full and evidenced understanding (such as that possessed by an academic researching matter and the properties of matter). Gaining more knowledge may improve the degree of understanding you have, but it does not mean that you will necessarily be able to put all the facts together to create a high degree of understanding.

Table 7.1   Forms of Knowledge

Form of Knowledge	Description
Factual knowledge	As the name implies, it is simply the acquisition of facts. China is in Asia; Fe is the symbol for Iron; Queen Victoria was born in 1819 etc. It is the discrete knowledge associated with a discipline, subject or topic. It includes technical terms and it can be isolated, i.e. the facts stand independently and do not rely on other connected facts.
Conceptual knowledge	Interrelated knowledge, i.e. facts that are dependent on other facts, may combine to form conceptual knowledge. They are the basic elements of larger structures of knowledge. For example, a child may learn that the plural form of a word can be formed by adding an 's' to the original word. It is the form of knowledge that characterises concepts or principles. It requires reflection and experience.
Procedural knowledge	Procedural knowledge is the knowledge that is required to complete a task, e.g. knowing how to change a punctured tyre on a car requires procedural knowledge, as does knowing how to create a dovetail joint in carpentry. It is the type of knowledge used in the performance of a task.
Metacognitive knowledge	This is 'knowing about knowing': it is the sort of knowledge that is necessary for someone to know what strategies they should use to solve a problem or how to learn a new skill or acquire new knowledge.

If we reconfigure Bloom's cognitive taxonomy and add in the idea that knowledge comes in various forms, then we have a way of combining his taxonomy with an understanding of the importance of knowledge in developing understanding alongside other skills, such as application, synthesis and creativity. This is what Krathwohl (2002) did in devising a two dimensional framework for knowledge and cognitive processes (see Table 7.2).

Table 7.2 Forms of knowledge and Bloom's cognitive process dimensions (after Krathwohl, 2002)

Form of Knowledge	Bloom's Cognitive Domain Dimensions					
	Remember	Understand	Apply	Analyse	Evaluate	Create
Factual knowledge						
Conceptual knowledge						
Procedural knowledge						
Metacognitive knowledge						

(Source: A Revision of Bloom's Taxonomy: An Overview, David R. Krathwohl, Nov 1, 2002, Taylor & Francis, reprinted by permission of the publisher (Taylor & Francis Ltd, http://www.tandfonline.com))

As Krathwohl (2002 p.218) says, the reconfigured Bloom's taxonomy is a much more useful way 'to classify objectives, activities, and assessments [as it] provides a clear, concise, visual representation of a particular course or unit'. It is also a useful way to classify the knowledge claims of research and analyse research reports and papers.

Critical reading and writing

The essence of critical reading is the ability to identify what is opinion and what is argument. Put simply, an opinion is a statement made without any real evidence. It may contain facts, it may read like an argument for or against something, but it will not have what is technically known as a 'warranted' conclusion. In other words, there is no reasoning (no warrant) that leads to a valid conclusion.

In critical reading the objective is to identify and sort out what is opinion and what is a valid argument. From there you will need to look at the conclusions made for each argument and decide whether those conclusions are warranted or unwarranted. It is not uncommon to come across incomplete or flawed arguments in your reading. The ability to identify such arguments is something that comes with experience and practice. Wallace and Wray (2016 p.7) describe critical reading as:

> The skill … in assessing the extent to which authors have provided adequate justification for the claims they make. This assessment depends partly on what the authors have communicated and partly on other relevant knowledge, experience and inference that you are able to draw on.

Box 7.3 is an 'opinion' article on education. It contains arguments and opinions, but as you will see from the analysis of the article, it does not present warranted arguments that stand up to academic scrutiny even though it may contain facts.

BOX 7.3

MAKING SENSE OF IT

James Williams

Police relations with the public are so crucial

How does the author know this? There is no reference to any police, government or research publication to support this statement.

KNIFE crime is in the headlines. Families are being ripped apart as young people die needlessly on our streets.

Unlike guns, knives are much more difficult to control. The Government should do more to stop the importation and online sales of hunting knifes, and weapons which have no other purpose than to maim or kill. But we can't remove knives completely – even a small kitchen knife in the wrong hands becomes a lethal weapon.

The only solution is to attack the root of the problem – why do young people feel that they have to carry knives? Gang culture has increased in recent years and this coincides with a drastic reduction in police numbers and a police presence on the streets.

I'm not attacking the police and shifting the blame to them for not addressing knife crime. Police forces nationally are overwhelmed, underfunded and their resources stretched by the demands of modern society. It's not a matter of simply putting more police on the streets to reduce or eliminate knife crime. Things are never that simple.

More police are needed, not just for knife crime but to cover many other types of crime and antisocial behaviour. We need are more specialist police teams. We need them to tackle the rise in gang culture, the "county lines" problem of gangs recruiting vulnerable young people to deliver drugs and weapons from one county to another. We need a concerted effort to tackle the reasons why young people feel that a life within a gang is preferable to any other lifestyle.

If our only response to knife crime is the arrest and punishment of young people carrying knives we are failing. We fail the victims of knife crime, we fail the victim's family and we fail the perpetrator of that crime.

Knife crime is not an inner city problem or confined to poorer areas. It's a problem for each and every one of us. Even if we're secure that our family, our children, would never carry knives or be involved with gang culture, we cannot control what happens elsewhere.

As a child in the 60s I recall the visit of police officers to my school for a range of things. There was road safety, Billy the Belisha Beacon who taught us to look right, look left, then look right again, before crossing the road. Something I still do 50 years later. The police also ran cycling proficiency training. We saw the police as trusted friends and protectors not enemies. I may be viewing this through

rose tinted glasses, but I cannot help wondering how we can build relationships and gain the trust of young people if they view current society as a police state where the police are the enemy. The fewer police we have, the fewer resources they have, the more they will only be able to attack the consequences of crime – arrest and punishment, not prevention.

The code of ethics for the police states that their mission is to prevent crime and protect the public. Their core function is to prevent crime and antisocial behaviour. They are tasked with keeping the peace, protecting and reassuring communities.

Sussex Police cover a huge area that includes rural parts and farmland, small villages, towns and cities, and an international airport that has 39 million people pass through it each year. They pledge to serve and protect more than 1.5 million Sussex residents and all on yearly reducing budgets. Since 2010 there have been cuts of more than £57 million imposed on Sussex Police. We've already seen that many minor offences are not ful-

Knife crime is not just an inner city problem or confined to poor areas

ly investigated, especially when the chance of finding the culprit is very low. This gives out the wrong message – that low level crime is OK, a theft here, a burglary there.

I'm not advocating we return to Dixon of Dock Green times where the local bobby would know everyone's business and give the local tearaway a clip around the ear for chalking on a wall. But I do think we need to address the root cause of knife crime. Young people often carry knives, they say, for protection. It's that fear we need to tackle and that comes from getting into the heart of gang culture that instils such fear. What drives gang culture is often drugs and petty crime, a theft here a burglary there, to prove your "credentials" to join the gang. Preventing and tackling low level crime is important.

Children don't go from no crime to murderous gang member overnight. Low level crime is a road to higher crime and we need to fund our police to set up a roadblock, prevent and protect, not merely mop up the blood after the crime has been committed. The roadblock begins with good police community relationships.

(Continued)

• How does the author know this? There is no reference to any police, government or research publication to support this statement.	Knife crime is in the headlines. Families are being ripped apart as young people die needlessly on our streets. Unlike guns, knives are much more difficult to control. The government should do more to stop the importation and online sales of hunting knives, and weapons which have no other purpose than to maim or kill. But we can't remove knives completely – even a small kitchen knife in the wrong hands becomes a lethal weapon.	
	The only solution is to attack the root of the problem – why do young people feel that they have to carry knives? Gang culture has increased in recent years and this coincides with a drastic reduction in police numbers and a police presence on the streets.	• There is no cited evidence here, but the author is making a common assumption.
• Another sweeping statement with no reference to any statistics to back up the claim.	I'm not attacking the police and shifting the blame to them for not addressing knife crime. Police forces nationally are overwhelmed, underfunded and their resources stretched by the demands of modern society. It's not a matter of simply putting more police on the streets to reduce or eliminate knife crime. Things are never that simple.	
	More police are needed, not just for knife crime but to cover many other types of crime and antisocial behaviour. We need more specialist police teams. We need are (sic) them to tackle the rise in gang culture, the 'county lines' problem of gangs recruiting vulnerable young people to deliver drugs, weapons etc. from one county to another. We need a concerted effort to tackle the reasons why young people feel that a life within a gang is preferable to any other lifestyle.	

If our only response to knife crime is the arrest and punishment of young people carrying knives we are failing. We fail the victims of knife crime, we fail the victim's family and we fail the perpetrator of that crime.

Knife crime is not an inner-city problem or confined to poorer areas. It's a problem for each and every one of us. Even if we're secure that our family, our children, would never carry knives or be involved with gang culture, we cannot control what happens elsewhere.

As a child in the 60s I recall the visit of police officers to my school for a range of things. There was road safety, Billy the belisha beacon who taught us to look right, look left, then look right again, before crossing the road. Something I still do 50 years later. The police also ran cycling proficiency training. We saw the police as trusted friends and protectors not enemies. I may be viewing this through rose-tinted glasses, but I cannot help wondering how we can build relationships and gain the trust of young people if they view current society as a police state where the police are the enemy. The fewer police we have, the fewer resources they have, the more they will only be able to attack the consequences of crime – arrest and punishment, not prevention. The code of ethics for the police states that their mission is to prevent crime and protect the public. Their core function is to prevent crime and anti-social behaviour. They are tasked with keeping the peace, and protecting and reassuring communities.

- This is a personal anecdote; it may be true but that does not mean it applies universally or even generally. It's very specific to the author's experience.

(Continued)

• These are factual statements based on police data. Even though there is no citation, they could be easily checked.	Sussex police cover a huge area that includes rural parts and farmland, small villages, towns and cities, and an international airport that has 39 million people pass through it each year. They pledge to serve and protect over 1.5 million Sussex residents and all on yearly reducing budgets. Since 2010 there have been cuts of more than £57 million imposed on Sussex police. We've already seen that many minor offences are not fully investigated, especially when the chance of finding the culprit is very low. This gives out the wrong message – that low level crime is OK – a theft here, a burglary there.	
	I'm not advocating we return to Dixon of Dock Green times where the local bobby would know everyone's business and give the local tearaway a clip around the ear for chalking on a wall. But I do think we need to address the root cause of knife crime. Young people often carry knives, they say, for protection. It's that fear we need to tackle and that comes from getting into the heart of gang culture that instils such fear.	• This is an emotional appeal to older people who recall the TV programme and the 'gentle' way crime and policing was portrayed.
• This is pure rhetoric, an appeal for action, the use of a metaphor and a common figure of speech – the 'roadblock' – as a means to persuade people that 'something needs to be done'.	What drives gang culture is often drugs and petty crime, a theft here a burglary there, to prove your 'credentials' to join the gang. Preventing and tackling low level crime is important. Children don't go from no crime to murderous gang member overnight. Low level crime is a road to higher crime and we need to fund our police to set up a roadblock, prevent and protect, not merely mop up the blood after the crime has been committed. The roadblock begins with good police community relationships.	

Reproduced with kind permission from *The Argus*

Critical writing is the application of critical reading to your own writing, i.e. knowing what is an opinion and what is a warranted argument. If you can critically read a text, then you should be able to apply this to your own writing and be able to write critically. As Wallace and Wray (2016 p.7) put it:

> The skill of critical writing lies in convincing your readers to accept your claims. You achieve their acceptance through the effective communication of adequate reasons and evidence for these claims.

In critical reading and writing it is useful to be able to identify flawed arguments. Table 7.3 sets out a range of flaws that can be commonly found. The table shows how to identify a flaw, provides a real-life example, and then puts forward key questions that as a reader you should ask. The final column provides an example of how the 'flaw' could be resolved. The table comes from a book on critical reading and writing for postgraduate students by Wallace and Wray (2016).

Table 7.3   Identifying flaws in arguments (adapted from Wallace and Wray, 2016 p.41)

Type of argument flaw	Example of the flaw in text	Questions to ask to check whether there is a flaw	How the flaw could be resolved in the text
Unwarranted conclusion	The best musicians make the worst teachers.	Why do you think that? How do you know?	The eye for fine detail possessed by the best musicians tends to make them over-critical and discouraging with pupils. (with citation to support this statement)
Warrant apparent, but no conclusion	Johnson's research shows that people often sign legal documents without reading them. Legal documents can be difficult to read.	So what? What do these different pieces of evidence, if taken together, imply?	People may fail to read legal documents because they are too difficult.
Warrant in place, but an illogical conclusion	People in English-speaking countries tend not to know another language. This indicates they are poor language learners.	Is this the only possible conclusion? Are there other, more plausible conclusions or other equally viable alternative conclusions?	This may suggest that English speakers do not see the need to know other languages. Other reasons could be related to the lack of languages on offer in schools.
Conclusion not linked to any warrant(s)	Statistics show that teenagers are drinking too much to be good for their health. Alcoholic drinks should be increased in price.	What causal relationship between the amount of alcohol consumed and the price are you suggesting?	Since teenagers are more likely to have limited access to funds, raising the price of alcohol may result in less alcohol being consumed by teenagers.

(Continued)

Table 7.3   (Continued)

Type of argument flaw	Example of the flaw in text	Questions to ask to check whether there is a flaw	How the flaw could be resolved in the text
Conclusion with inadequate warrant(s)	Trainee managers learn more effectively when they are praised than when their efforts are criticised. In a survey of female trainee managers in a retail company, 77% said they liked to be praised.	Is the evidence adequate to justify the extent of the claim? Is the evidence appropriately interpreted? What is the link between 'liking to be praised' and learning more effectively?	However, males and females may respond differently to praise.

When you identify flaws in the arguments made by others, you need to expose these in your writing or summaries of those arguments. Just as there are ways in which arguments can be flawed, there are also ways in which, when responding to arguments, a rebuttal can also be flawed. Such flawed arguments are also called 'logical fallacies' – there are many of them, too many to cover in detail here, but some of the most common are set out in Table 7.4. Critical reading and writing require you to be aware of these flaws and fallacies; they help in analysing the work of others as well as ensuring your own writing cannot be criticised for including flawed arguments and logical fallacies.

Table 7.4   Common logical fallacies

Logical fallacy	Common description	Example
Ad hominem	Attacking the person rather than the argument they make	What would you know about teaching? When was the last time you taught a class of 30 children on a regular basis? It's clear you were not a good teacher as you left the classroom to work elsewhere.
Argumentum ad ignorantiam	An appeal from ignorance, assuming that a claim is either false or true, because the actual claim has not yet been proven false or true.	Nobody can explain how life began, therefore the answer is that life began as a result of the divine intervention of a supernatural being.
Argumentum ad nauseam	An argument put forward so often that people do not question it anymore, and simply accept the argument without supporting evidence.	The government repeatedly states that 'more money than ever is being put into England's schools': this claim is made repeatedly but ignores the supporting evidence that numbers of children have increased significantly.
Argumentum e silentio	An argument made from the absence of evidence rather than the from the evidence itself.	'Although the insecticides were dumped in the sea, there are no known harmful effects on marine life.' The problem here is, nobody has ever tested whether the chemicals do have any effect on marine life as they were never intended to be used or disposed of in the sea.

Logical fallacy	Common description	Example
Argument from incredulity	An argument based on the disbelief of the holder – 'I don't believe it, therefore it cannot be true'.	I cannot imagine how humans evolved from single-celled organisms, therefore it cannot be true, and evolution is a lie.
Circular reasoning	When the argument begins by stating what the person wants to prove anyway.	I don't deserve to have a detention for talking in the lesson as other children were also talking.
False dichotomy	The putting forward of two statements as the only possible statements to choose from when other solutions may well be possible.	Donald Trump is a 'master' of the false dichotomy. His insistence in building a wall to separate the US and Mexico results in the false dichotomy that anyone who opposes the wall is in favour of completely open borders and uncontrolled immigration.
Moving the goal posts	When evidence that disproves a position is dismissed, or taken as read, and other evidence is requested that is more demanding.	When teacher A is observed and has met all their previous targets, but on this occasion there is no recognition of the improvement. Instead new, previously satisfactory elements of the lesson are highlighted as inadequate and a cause for concern that will prevent promotion or advancement.
Red herring	When the proponent of an argument tries to distract the audience by introducing something that is irrelevant to the original argument, but much easier to prove.	As a teacher, you catch a student cheating on a test. As a protest the student says, 'I only cheated because my parents expect me to do well and I didn't want to let them down'. This is a red herring meant to divert attention away from the act of cheating, which the student knows is wrong.
Straw man	The act of misrepresenting your opponent's position and then attacking that false position.	A headteacher gives out a difficult task to pupils that results in poor scores overall. One teacher says in a staff meeting that perhaps due to the level of difficulty of the task those who completed it should be given a few marks as extra credit.
		The headteacher's rebuttal is that giving all the students a perfect mark for no reason means that children will not work hard in the future. This rebuttal distorts the teacher's argument. There was no request for every student to receive a perfect score, let alone extra marks, and a reason was given for some to have extra marks.

Summary

Being critical is not about passing judgement on others. The process of criticality can be a positive as well as negative. It is not simply about finding fault. There is a high degree of nuance necessary. Things are not always 'right' or 'wrong'. Criticality involves the use of a reasoned, expert, articulate examination of the ideas and methods provided and used by others, to come to conclusions about what they have been studying and reporting on. If anything, criticality looks at the quality of an argument or conclusion, rather than the qualities of the person. Key parts of being a good critical thinker are identifying the arguments being made, formulating an interrogation, and using specific questions to test the veracity of the arguments. If you are reading research with a view to informing your own study, then it is essential that you consider carefully the research questions you have and then ascertain whether any research you read is relevant and pertinent.

The next chapter provides a six-step process for critical analysis. This guides you through the process and gives a framework for reading research.

Further reading

Chatfield, T. (2017) *Critical Thinking: Your Guide to Effective Argument, Successful Analysis and Independent Study* London: Sage

This is an accessible and comprehensive guide to critical thinking. It introduces aspects of logic, rhetoric, bias and reasoning.

Wallace, M., & Wray, A. (2016) *Critical Reading and Writing for Postgraduates* London: Sage

This book has a range of techniques and strategies to help you improve your critical reading and writing skills. It uses actual research which is then deconstructed to help you understand the process of criticality.

Bibliography

Achinstein, P. (1983) *The Nature of Explanation* Oxford: Oxford University Press on Demand

Chatfield, T. (2017) *Critical Thinking: Your Guide to Effective Argument, Successful Analysis and Independent Study* London: Sage

Grimm, S.R. (2006) Is understanding a species of knowledge? *British Journal for the Philosophy of Science* Vol.57 No.3 pp.515–535

Krathwohl, D.R. (2002) A revision of Bloom's taxonomy: an overview *Theory into Practice* Vol.41 No.4 pp.212–218

Kvanvig, J.L. (2003) *The Value of Knowledge and the Pursuit of Understanding* Cambridge: Cambridge University Press

Lipton, P. (2003) *Inference to the Best Explanation* Abingdon: Routledge

Pritchard, D. (2014) Knowledge and understanding. In Fairweather, A. (ed.) *Virtue Epistemology Naturalized: Bridges Between Virtue Epistemology and Philosophy of Science* pp.315–327 Cham: Springer

Wallace, M., & Wray, A. (2016) *Critical Reading and Writing for Postgraduates* London: Sage

Zagzebski, L. (2017) What is knowledge? In Greco, J. & Sosa, E. (eds) *The Blackwell Guide to Epistemology* Vol.1 pp.92–116 Oxford: Blackwell

8

A Critical Analysis Framework

Chapter aims

- To be familiar with a framework for critical analysis
- To apply the framework to published research
- To see the framework in action

Introduction

Chapter 7 defined and explored what is meant by criticality. This chapter examines a framework for critical analysis. When you are reading research, or any professional writing on education, it is helpful to have a framework in mind for critically analysing and recording your thoughts about the quality of the arguments and evidence being used.

The framework provides prompts for key questions to ask about the quality and rigour of the work under consideration. It will assess the methodological approach and the methods used (how relevant and appropriate they are), as well as asking questions about the conclusions drawn and whether the evidence supports the conclusions.

It may well be that not all the steps will apply to all the research or professional items you read. The framework proposed can be adapted for use and amended to fit more comfortably with the type of research you are reading.

In the first part of the chapter the framework for critical analysis will be described. A published research article is then analysed using the framework.

The six-step process of critical analysis

The six-step process described below has been devised from reading and distilling the key actions from several approaches to critical analysis. The process is not rigid and can be adapted to suit a wide range of types of research and scholarly work.

Step1: Identify the intention

A good writer will strive to ensure that the intention of their text is clear. There is a lot to be said for the old adage of tell the reader what you want to say, say it, and then remind them in your summary what you said. For research papers published in journals, the abstract, which summarises the key points and findings, should do this job quickly and efficiently. When deciding what research to read and what research would contribute to your knowledge of a topic, reading the abstract is the fastest way to prioritise what requires more detailed reading and what can be discarded. Like most things, a binary choice of 'in' or 'out' is unlikely. You are going to come across work that does not easily fit a category. It is worthwhile therefore to divide your reading into three categories: that which certainly requires more detailed reading and analysis; that which can easily be discarded as not relevant; and that which requires more consideration before it can be included or discarded.

Once you have some work to review, you will need to understand what sort of research is being presented. It's worth asking the following questions:

Is the research …

- quantitative, qualitative or mixed methods?
- an empirical study?
- action research?
- a case study or studies?
- a meta-review, meta-analysis or meta-study?

Having established the type of research that you're looking at, the next thing to do is to think about what the research is trying to tell you, i.e. its intent. Is it describing something new? Perhaps it could be a new and different approach to teaching. Is the research describing the 'particular' or the 'general'? Some studies are designed to be generalisable, others only describe a particular situation. It could be that the research is proposing a new theory, or it is modifying or adding to existing theory?

Some research, such as meta-reviews and meta-analyses, sets out to combine results from previously published research into one paper. The intent of this type of research is to formulate a considered view of the evidence that currently exists either in favour of or against a position or theory.

Before you begin to delve into the papers and research that you have collected you must be clear on what the researcher's intent is, as this will guide you in your appraisal of the methodology and methods used and will help you understand how rigorous the paper is, as well as give you indications about the validity of the evidence.

Step 2: Identify the main ideas

Identifying the main ideas in a good research paper should be relatively easy. Ideally, the research questions will be clearly set out in one of the first few sections of the paper. If not, then the researcher will pose the questions at various intervals during the paper. There is also the conclusion section where the main ideas will once again be articulated. If you are struggling to identify the main ideas, that may tell you something about the quality of the article you are reading.

Step 3: Identify the underlying theoretical and methodological approaches

If there is a methodology section, it's normally here that you find the theoretical approach taken by the researcher. This should let you know the epistemological and ontological basis of the research, and it will allow you to understand how it fits with your own epistemological and ontological approach.

The methods used to collect, analyse and describe the data should also be set out, ideally stating why the various methods were chosen and why they are the best methods for this research. It is often in this area that criticality can be most successfully applied. If the methods used are not suitable, then this could call into question the results (see Box 8.1).

BOX 8.1 LOADED AND LEADING QUESTIONS IN SURVEYS

Any methods used in research must be rigorous and appropriate. Often, weaknesses in research will show in the methods chosen and used. Questionnaires are a common method of gathering data, but a poorly constructed questionnaire will lead to poor research.

'Have you stopped beating your child yet?'

Surveys are very difficult to construct: whether you ask questions in person or construct an online survey, getting the question wording right is one of the most important things to do to ensure that the data you gather are good, unbiased data.

Loaded questions, such as the question posed in the heading above, are some of the worst types of questions you see in surveys. There are also leading questions which, while not as obvious as loaded questions, are still methodologically very poor.

The question 'Have you stopped beating your child yet?' presupposes that the child is being beaten by you. If you are restricted to a 'yes or no' answer you lose. Say yes and it implies you used to beat your child. Say no and it implies you are currently beating your child. It is a classic no-win situation. While the question posed in the heading is ridiculous, some loaded questions are more difficult to spot.

Consider the following questions, which may be asked in relation to schools. Superficially they may seem appropriate, but they are, in fact, loaded:

1. What do you think are the three main causes of bad behaviour in comprehensive schools?
2. Do you think that a partisan political ideology should drive government policy on education?
3. Should politicians interfere with headteachers' autonomy over the exclusion of violent children?

In all three cases above the questions are heavily loaded.

In question 1 there is a presumption that bad behaviour happens in comprehensive schools, whereas all other types of schools, such as grammar schools, private schools etc. have been excluded from the question. In question 2 there is a presumption that government policy will be partisan and ideological: it does not specify whether that ideology is right, left or centre, but it presupposes that no government policy will be neutral. Question 3 specifically implies that politicians may be planning to prevent exclusions (but provides no evidence for this) and it presumes this to be an attack on headteacher autonomy.

Leading questions

Loaded questions can often be easily spotted, but leading questions can be very subtle. Leading questions will steer the person responding to the question to arrive at a particular answer, one that perhaps suits the bias of the questioner:

1. Would you naturally agree or disagree that the exclusion of children from schools, e.g. for violent behaviour, should be decided by a headteacher?
2. What improvement in grades do you predict for next year's GCSE cohort?
3. Do you regularly have problems with Year 8 set 2?

In question 1 the example given is an extreme one (violent behaviour) and is a presumption that nobody would disagree that violent children should be excluded, hence the 'naturally agree' versus an unqualified 'disagree'. In question 2 the assumption is that a cohort will achieve a 'better' set of results regardless of their prior attainment. For question 3 there is an assumption that the teacher has problems already with Year 8 set 2, so it's a matter of how bad the problems are or how regularly they occur.

Learning to recognise loaded and leading questions is a good way of assessing the quality of data collected via questionnaires, surveys, or even interviews.

Step 4: What evidence is presented to support the arguments?

How does the author support their main argument(s)? What evidence do they provide (qualitative or quantitative)? Is the evidence strong evidence or weak? In this step the quality of the evidence can also be assessed. Evidence can be graded as high quality, moderate quality, low quality and very low quality. From a scientific standpoint, high-quality evidence will come from things like randomised controlled trials or measurements that are both accurate and precise. Low- and very low-quality evidence may come from casual observations, anecdotes, or poorly gathered/recorded evidence (e.g. with no contextual data or with no indication of where the data come from). Determining the quality of evidence will also require knowledge of the study as a whole. For example, the quality rating you may give for evidence could be downgraded due to any limitations in the design of the study, problems in the implementation of the methods, variability in the results obtained, any bias found within the published study. Likewise, the quality of the evidence could be improved if there is a large dataset and any potential biases have been identified, described and taken into account.

Step 5: The 'so what?' test

Why does this research matter? This is the 'so what?' question. Why should we care? What are consequences of this research if it's taken seriously and influences policy and/or practice? The 'so what?' test must consider the wider implications of any study. Could it be useful to, or apply in, different contexts or in different countries/cultures? Having a study that is so specific it can only be of use within a very tightly bound context may not be of any use at all. You have to ask what the purpose of such a study is, why do it, and why report on it, if it cannot have any application in different contexts. This test is an important one when looking for research for a literature review. If a study is very good, but does not add anything to your research questions, it will not merit a place in your literature review. All the time you are reading research you will need to be going back to the notion of why you need the research you are reading (in other words, how does it relate to your research questions) and how it will add to your overall understanding. If it does neither then you will need to reject the research; if it does one or the other, it's worth looking again and seeing whether the other question could be applied.

Step 6: What questions does the article prompt?

Is anything in the article unclear? Is there something the author(s) failed to consider? What would you ask the author(s) if you had the opportunity? Are ethical considerations adequately covered? Good research will prompt the reader to consider further questions. The best research will either pose further related questions or indicate where there is more research to do or different avenues to investigate.

This six-step process provides a framework for critical engagement with research. It can be applied to a wide range of materials from articles to books, even podcasts and video. The rest of the chapter applies the process to a piece of published academic research in education. The article will be critically analysed using the six-step process so that you can see this in action.

Applying the six-step process to published research

The article being analysed, *Neuromyths in education: prevalence and predictors of misconceptions among teachers* (Dekker et al., 2012), is an open access article (i.e. it is freely accessible to read/download) that was published in the journal *Frontiers in Psychology* on October 18th 2012. You can obtain a full copy of the article from the following web address: https://doi.org/10.3389/fpsyg.2012.00429

Step 1: Identify the intention

The abstract of the paper contains the key intention for the research. The authors 'investigated the prevalence and predictors of neuromyths among teachers in selected regions of the United Kingdom and the Netherlands'. The abstract states why the authors thought the study was worth doing. The writers characterise misconceptions about the brain as 'so-called "neuromyths" … that may have adverse effects on educational practice' (Abstract: p.1). The abstract goes on to briefly describe how the study was carried out and what the key findings were.

Step 2: Identify the main ideas

The Introduction to the paper provides the main ideas associated with the study. It summarises what research exists on this issue and why the study is needed. It is one long justification for the study and sets out why such a study is needed and why it is important.

The Introduction sets out some key facts:

- Teachers are interested in neuroscience.
- There is a gap between what we know in neuroscience and how it applies in education, which leads to misconceptions.
- At the time the paper was published not much research had been done into the prevalence of neuromyths among education professionals.

At this point the authors then introduce a testable idea or hypothesis:

- If teachers who are interested in neuroscience believe 'neuromyths' they could implement 'wrong' ideas into their practice as teachers.

Following on from establishing the main ideas, the authors then add other intentions: 1) to see whether there is a difference between what UK teachers believe compared to teachers from the Netherlands; 2) to see whether there are any 'identifying factors' that could lead to being able to predict which teachers may believe in neuromyths. In this section of the article there may also be some discussion of any existing research that is similar to the work being reported on, or any work that may be relevant to the study being described. For example, the authors outline a study examining neuroscience knowledge in the general population of Brazil, and a study showing that neuromyths were prevalent among Initial Teacher Training (ITT) students. They also cited some interesting research showing that people are more likely to 'believe research findings when they are accompanied by brain images and neuroscience explanations, even when these are incorrect' (Introduction: p.2).

Step 3: Identify the underlying theoretical and methodological approaches

Some of the information for this step is included in the introduction to the article. In different journals this information may be set out in a section entitled 'Methodology'. Other journals will have different requirements for authors, specifying how they should set out their work. What will be common is the authors setting out any theories that underpin their work or any theoretical approach they are bringing to their work.

In this article the authors set out what they did in a section called 'Materials and Methods'. They state how many participants there were and where they were drawn from geographically, and they describe the main characteristics of the participants, e.g. age profile, gender, age range they taught, etc. This is all good standard practice. They further describe the data-gathering instrument (a questionnaire which is included as an appendix). In a section called 'Data Analysis' they describe how they processed the results and what statistical models they used. Questions that arise from reading this section include:

- Is the method described appropriate?
- Are the questions asked in the survey going to deliver an answer to the main research questions?
- Are there any loaded or leading questions?
- What does the description of the participants tell us about the sampling technique used (e.g. is it serendipitous? Designed to be representative?)
- Are the data analysis techniques appropriate?
- Are there enough data to reliably run the statistical tests proposed?

The use of statistics can occasionally provide a veneer of rigour and validity to studies. For example, one of my favourite 'statistical jokes' summarises a key issue when reporting statistics. In a clinical trial – involving mice – of a new drug aimed at curing cancer, one third of the test subjects lived, while a third died. Unfortunately, the other one escaped and ran away.

A sample of three is obviously ridiculous, but proper sampling is difficult to get right. Get it wrong and you can prove almost anything you wish.

Step 4: What evidence is presented to support the key arguments?

The evidence presented in the Dekker et al. (2012) paper consists of the results of processing the responses to the questionnaire by the 242 participants. The evidence is based on statistical analyses which looked to see whether there were any predictors for belief in neuromyths. It simply calculated whether the teachers from the different countries had any belief in various pseudoscientific ideas about the brain and learning, and then it tested to see whether having prior knowledge or interest in how the brain works makes it more or less likely that they would accept or believe in various brain myths. To understand exactly how the results are being interpreted by the authors, you will need to read the 'Discussion' section thoroughly and then think carefully about the arguments made and the evidence used to back up the arguments.

Step 5: The 'so what?' test

The essence of this step is to take the arguments and the results being presented, and simply ask yourself what difference this makes to our knowledge and understanding of the issue being investigated. In this paper there is an interesting question that could add to our knowledge of the prevalence of neuromyths in education – are teachers in different countries affected in the same way? When it comes to the acceptance of neuromyths, do they believe the same things? Are neuromyths as prevalent in the Netherlands as they may appear to be in the UK? This article passes the 'so what?' test in that it is looking at something that is relevant and could add to the body of knowledge that we have on this subject.

Step 6: What questions does the article prompt?

Superficially the study on neuromyths is sound – the statistical tests are good, the results are clearly set out; but there are problems. The main problem, in my view, is the limited sample size. Overall there were 242 teachers who responded. This number was drawn from several areas in the Netherlands, but only one region in the UK, i.e. Dorset.

The number of primary schools in the Netherlands in 2011 (the most likely year when the data were gathered) was 7,434 and there were 645 secondary schools. Overall there were approximately 125,000 primary teachers and 83,000 secondary teachers (Missler and Groeneveld, 2014). The teachers who responded to this survey in the Netherlands constitute a small sample – about 0.05% of all primary and secondary teachers. There is nothing in the paper to indicate that the sample was one that was selected to be representative of all the teachers; it was seen as 'random'.

For the UK participants, there were 137 teachers, all from one UK region – Dorset. This is the opposite of what happened in the Netherlands (where several regions supplied participants). Taking all the teachers from one region cannot be representative of the profession as a whole (I must point out here that the paper does not claim that its sample is representative, but as you will see later, how the results can be reported by others may give this impression). The authors consider the sample to be a 'random selection', as noted earlier, but how random? The authors would have a good case to say that this is 'random' for the Netherlands sample, but is it random for the UK sample where all the teachers come from one geographic region?

In England in 2011 there were 438,000 full-time equivalent teachers in England, with nearly 195,000 in mainstream nursery and primary schools and 138,000 mainstream secondary teachers; the balance of teachers came from special schools and academies, or were being centrally employed by local authorities (Department for Education and Employment (DfEE), 2012). As is apparent, the sample of 137 teachers from Dorset is even smaller given the much larger number of teachers in the UK, when compared to the Netherlands – 0.03% of teachers in England.

Immediately the size of the sample, where it was drawn from and how it was compiled rule out being able to generalise about the findings or extrapolate to the whole population of teachers.

How was this study subsequently reported?

The problem with the study looked at above is not with its methods, and not even with the structure of the paper or how it was put together – it lies in how it is being reported elsewhere. For example, a paper published in the same journal – *Frontiers in Psychology*, in 2017 (Newton and Miah, 2017) – stated that 'A 2012 study demonstrated that 93% of schoolteachers in the UK agree with the statement "Individuals learn better when they receive information in their preferred Learning Style (e.g., auditory, visual, kinaesthetic) (Dekker et al., 2012)"'. It may have demonstrated that 93% of the sample of 137 Dorset teachers agreed with the statement, but to extrapolate and say that 93% of UK teachers agree is simply wrong. The UK includes Wales, Scotland and Northern Ireland – no teachers from these countries were included in the study, and it's based on a single region in England. This is a poor interpretation of what the study actually found. A quick Google search shows that this spurious figure pops up in other articles and online blogs. It has the potential to become an 'accepted' figure even though a brief critical analysis of the source material shows that such an interpretation is at best unreliable, and at worst a complete fabrication that could damage the standing of not just UK teachers but teachers in the Netherlands as well.

Numbers and figures like this spurious '93%' have the ability to percolate and permeate the discourse around what teachers 'believe'. It can present a very false impression of reality. If we visited a secondary school in England, with a staff of 100, would 93 of them really report that they 'believed' in learning styles?

The lesson from how this study was reported is to be sceptical of the facts and figures you read, even if they appear to be backed with references. A statement attributing a belief to over 90% of all teachers is, in some ways, extraordinary, and one that requires some extraordinary or very robust and rigorous evidence. A sceptical view of research should encourage you to track down original articles and check that the author's interpretation is a good one.

Summary

What is presented in this chapter is not the 'only' way to analyse critically any research you read – it is one possible way. It sets out a stepped and staged process which forms a useful framework for critical analysis. The key watchword for any critical analysis is scepticism; do not simply accept what you read. You must think about what is being presented, and when facts and figures are presented ask yourself are these believable? In reading any research you have to ensure that the steps from raw data to final answer are logical.

What this chapter also illustrates is the problem of accepting secondary interpretations of the work of others. A properly peer-reviewed and published article provides a reader with confidence that what is presented is reliable, accurate and 'true'. But as has been shown here, just because something is written in an academic paper this does not mean that the writer's interpretation of other research is always correct. This gets us to the crux of the issue in reading research – are we reading the primary research or someone else's interpretation? If it is someone else's interpretation, can we trust it? It is far too easy (and far too common) for a study to be misrepresented and an urban myth created. Wherever possible we should always try to track down the original research and check that what is being reported is actually what was being said, whether the interpretation is correct and can be supported by the evidence presented. The further reading at the end of this chapter concentrates on books that explore and explode some of the more common myths about learning. The reason for these recommendations is that they provide a good guide to how others have critically evaluated evidence.

Further reading

Christodoulou, D. (2014) *Seven Myths About Education* Abingdon: Routledge
A concise refutation of some key, but misunderstood ideas in education.

De Bruyckere, P., Kirschner, P.A., & Hulshof, C.D. (2015) *Urban Myths About Learning and Education* Waltham, MA: Academic Press

This is a very accessible book that addresses several myths in teaching and learning.

Von Hippel, P.T. (2019) Is summer learning loss real? How I lost faith in one of education research's classic results *Education Next* Vol.19 No.4 pp 8–14

A detailed critical analysis of a 'classic' piece of research. It questions the summer 'loss' of learning experienced by children.

Bibliography

Dekker, S., Lee, N.C., Howard-Jones, P., & Jolles, J. (2012) Neuromyths in education: prevalence and predictors of misconceptions among teachers *Frontiers in Psychology* Vol. 3 pp 429–436

Department for Education and Employment (DfEE) (2012) *Statistical First Release 06/2012 School Workforce in England: November 2011* London: DfEE

Missler, R., & Groeneveld, R. (2014) *Key Figures 2009-2013: Education, Culture and Science* The Hague: Dutch Ministry of Education, Culture and Science

Newton, P.M., & Miah, M. (2017) Evidence-based higher education – is the learning styles 'myth' important? *Frontiers in Psychology* Vol. 8 pp 444–452

9
Putting Research into Practice

Chapter aims

- Establish reasons for teaching being a 'profession' rather than a job
- Think about reasons for researching your own practice
- Define different ways of carrying out action research
- Consider the ethics of education research involving children, young adults and vulnerable people

Introduction

Anyone who has trained to teach at any level, from early years to teaching and learning in higher education, will be familiar with the idea of reflective practice. Reflecting on what you do, how you do it, and indeed why you do things in a certain way, is the sign of professionalism. Teaching is a profession; it is not just a job. The difference between doing a job and being a professional is important. This difference is why you can develop a career in teaching.

In this chapter we will look at the difference between a job and a profession. We will also look at the challenges of applying research in the classroom. ('Classroom' is used here in the generic sense of being somewhere where learning takes place. It does not have to be a room with tables, chairs, whiteboards or blackboards, and it could just as easily be a place such as an outdoor environment.)

Conducting your own research brings benefits, but may have many drawbacks. This chapter will briefly examine both of these. Finally it will consider the important role of ethics in researching children's and young people's learning.

Is teaching a job or a profession?

The definition of a job is an activity or task that is done, usually for payment. These may be 'one-off' tasks or activities, but they may be (and usually are) regular tasks and activities that are carried out. A job is a common way to earn a living and many people will, throughout their working lives, do more than one job. It is not uncommon for one person to have more than one job at the same time. Not all jobs are carried out for payment – some jobs can be voluntary. Jobs may also require different levels of qualifications or training.

A profession, on the other hand, has different characteristics. A major difference between a job and a profession is that the latter will have a specialised body of knowledge that will have a theoretical basis. To enter a profession rather than just do a job means that professional training is required with certain standards, set by the profession, met. Meeting those standards will relate to the specialist body of knowledge, often by passing examinations or gaining a professional qualification. Other characteristics of a profession are that professionals bear greater responsibility for their work, due to their specialist knowledge. Often, accountability measures will be in place related to professional standards and/or outcomes. Professionals are expected to have a degree of independence and autonomy for the things that they do. In many professions, such as teaching, medicine etc., they also have a duty of care towards the people they interact with. Finally, professionals will also have a code of conduct or be bound by specific ethical constraints. They will be held to a higher standard of behaviour generally than those simply doing a job.

Being a professional will involve doing specific tasks (which may or may not need specialist knowledge) and of course teachers are paid. The rates of pay, as you would expect, tend to be greater for the qualified professional when compared to the unqualified person doing parts or aspects of the profession as specific jobs, e.g. being a cover supervisor in teaching. Being a professional also brings with it the chance of progression and promotion to higher levels of leadership – in other words, the ability to develop a career.

Teachers have, for many years, felt that their position as 'professionals' was not considered as comparable to other long-established and respected professions such as law and medicine. Part of this was due to the fact that both medicine and law have professional bodies that oversee the profession, and these bodies have considerable powers to regulate the profession and issue licences to practise. Their regulatory role meant that the professional bodies could, for example, suspend the right of a professional to practise, fine professionals for infringements of their professional duties, and require professionals to undergo further training in order to maintain their registration or licence to practise.

Sexton (2007) puts forward the idea that we can view teaching as a profession in two distinct ways. We can judge what teachers do against the types of activities that other professionals perform, and we can assess teachers against the norms of those professions. Alternatively, he says, 'research indicates that teachers view their professionalism in pragmatic, classroom-based terms rather than in terms of wider educational, philosophical or theoretical concerns'. This is his preferred way of viewing teachers as professionals. He goes on to argue that 'teachers must be more willing to engage with the "bigger issues" – /the moral, political, social and philosophical issues that shape the wider education agenda – /if they are to achieve the enhanced professional status they appear to desire' (Sexton, 2007 p.79).

How we prepare our teachers for entry and then enable them to progress during their early careers will also contribute to the idea of teaching being a profession rather than just being a job. Definitions of professionalism will vary, but there some general characteristics that we can agree are common to nearly all professions (as indicated above). These include responsibility, accountability, autonomy and ethical constraints.

One key aspect of professionalisation is the existence of a sound theoretical knowledge base. This means that access to the profession is guarded by having minimum standards for entry qualifications. In the UK, for example, teaching moved to a graduate-only profession in 1972. Prior to this, while teaching was 'certified', i.e. there was an expectation that teachers gained qualifications beyond university entry level, it was not a graduate-level profession. People who held undergraduate or postgraduate degrees could enter the profession without any further specialist training. That route into teaching still exists today, but only in the private sector (or, due to a change in the law post 2010, in academies) where there is no legal need for any further training or qualification. It has to be noted, however, that nearly all private schools, and certainly the vast majority of academies, do require some form of teacher training, if not on a formal basis then on an individual basis, school by school.

It's useful to look beyond the UK and consider how other countries prepare their teachers. Many countries have moved to teaching being a graduate profession. Nearly all will address subject knowledge, either as part of the training to be a teacher or by requiring an undergraduate subject degree followed by pedagogic training and training in child development. There will be a practical element, with trainee or pre-service teachers being affiliated to or placed in a school situation where they can gain practical experience of teaching, learning, assessing and curriculum planning. While many countries see teaching as a graduate occupation or profession, some will impose an even higher entry level (e.g. in Finland) where all teachers are qualified to Master's level. Worldwide there is a recognition that teaching should be a profession and that entry to that profession should begin at degree level. This is not universal however, as Darling-Hammond (2005 p.238) notes: 'some political forces oppose the professionalization of teaching and argue for reducing the "barriers to entry" posed by standards for preparation'.

It has been argued that the status of the teaching profession will vary from country to country (Hargreaves, 2009), with some well-known examples where the status of teachers is arguably more enhanced than in the UK, e.g. Japan and Finland. As noted earlier, in Finland entry to teaching is at full Master's level and applications for teacher training are very competitive. In the UK, while the Post Graduate Certificate in Education (PGCE) is at Master's level, it does not represent a full Master's degree and teachers are required only to have a Bachelor's degree (or equivalent) for entry to initial teacher education, or be on a degree course.

According to Price and Weatherby (2017) the Organisation for Economic Co-operation and Development (OECD) has provided a description of the input and output characteristics of teaching that gives us a measure of its status as a profession.

Table 9.1 Characteristics that define teaching as a profession (adapted from Price and Weatherby 2017)

Input Characteristics	Output Characteristics
Applicant quality	Working conditions
Applicant specialist knowledge and/or skills	Salary
Proportion of female applicants	Supply and demand
Preparation/initial teacher training	Career development and progress
Accountability and appraisal	Degree of working autonomy
Ease of access to professional development	Media reaction to the 'profession'
Concept of children as 'clients'	Governance and regulation (e.g. professional body)

Teachers as professionals have not, in the UK at least, been generally afforded the status of professionals that ranks alongside other professionals, such as lawyers and doctors. In part this is due to the long-standing lack of a coherent and single professional body that regulates teaching.

Professional regulation of teachers

The first attempt at forming a professional regulatory body for teachers was the General Teaching Council for England (GTCE), set up in 2000. It was disbanded at the stroke of a minister's pen in 2012 when Michael Gove was the appointed Secretary of State for Education in the relatively newly elected coalition government of 2010. As an imposed body, the GTCE was neither welcomed nor popular with teachers, who preferred to be represented by unions. The teachers' professional body had a troubled history and had been imposed without proper consultation. As the regulatory body, teachers were legally bound to be registered and to pay the GTCE fees. The GTCE held the active register of qualified teachers and had the power to award Qualified Teacher Status (QTS). Sister organisations such as the General Teaching Council for Scotland (GTCS) and for Northern Ireland (GTCNI) still exist, and regulate the profession in those countries, holding the list of qualified teachers, setting professional standards, hearing cases of alleged professional misconduct, and passing judgement on misconduct cases with options to suspend or revoke a person's entitlement to teach in the maintained sector. The General Teaching Council for Wales (GTCW) was replaced in 2015 with the Education Workforce Council, who oversee not only teachers but also associated support staff and youth workers etc.

Is teaching a profession or semi-profession?

Teachers will self-identify as professionals (Howsam, 1985), but there are significant problems with identifying teaching as a full profession equivalent to law and medicine. These problems revolve around the length and rigour of specialist training, a lack of true autonomy with respect to the practice of teaching, difficulties in identifying commonly held theoretical approaches to teaching, and differing requirements for the professional registration and licensing of teachers (Price and Weatherby, 2018). Most of the problems described above can easily be addressed, though it would be a major reform to review and lengthen initial teacher education. The second problem, the lack of a generally agreed theoretical base for the practice of teaching and a unified pedagogical approach, would be the most difficult to achieve. One major divide in teaching is between the 'traditionalist' direct instruction approach and the more 'progressive' child-centred inquiry approach. The need for an agreed set of professional requirements is, to a degree, met by the enforcement of the Teachers' Standards for QTS.

As these issues remain, it may be argued that, at best, teaching is currently a 'semi-profession'. The current drive for teaching and teachers to be more research-led and research-driven is a clear move that will help establish teaching as a full profession. The other problems, as noted above, will also need full attention. As Price and Weatherby (2018) set out, these can be addressed by establishing the following:

- professional benchmarks – initial standards plus 'progressions of learning';
- professional discretion – trust in the ability of teachers and greater autonomy;
- room for promotion – including success measures and reward structures;
- workplace conditions – organisational structures that enable teachers to perform well in their roles.

Researching your own practice

Researching your own practice as a teacher or educator brings many issues, not least that of the inherent possibility of bias that can lead to outcomes which ignore those things you may feel reflect badly or negatively on you. If the outcomes of your reflections or research are kept personal and not shared, you can often see negative aspects of your practice. Too often, people tend to be overly negative and critical of their own practice.

When I observe trainee teachers delivering lessons and we meet to discuss the feedback, invariably they will be quick to point out what they see as all the mistakes and problems. If I ask them to begin with three positive things they always struggle. The lesson from this with respect to researching your own practice is that any attempt to do so must be very carefully thought out and planned to ensure that any inherent bias is reduced, or better still, close to eliminated.

You need to understand the difference also between reflection and research. Reflecting on your practice should be a normal, everyday thing. No matter how much of a novice or experienced you are, the ability to reflect, as a professional, should be part and parcel of your normal work routine. Researching your own practice, however, is quite different and requires you to be an 'independent observer' of yourself, and this can take practice.

The three issues that impact most on researching your own practice are objectivity, reliability and validity (Clark-Wilson, 2008). Overcoming these issues means you must be, as a minimum, methodical in your research. But being methodical is not enough. You could, for example, set up a research regime and follow that methodically (see Figure 9.1). Simply following the steps of the action research cycle will not guarantee a high-quality outcome. What must happen at each stage is a process of thinking about and critically evaluating the evidence produced. Put simply, you need to go beyond looking at the data or results of your research and see what patterns and meaning emerge from it.

Action research

A common form of research done in schools is action research. There are a number of different forms of action research ranging from small-scale individual research undertaken by one teacher on an aspect (or aspects) of his or her own practice, to collaborative action research, participatory and non-participatory research, and collective action research.

Many students studying for a Master's degree, or as part of their Initial Teacher Training, will undertake single, participatory action research in fulfilment of part of their qualification. This usually involves researching an aspect of their practice or something related to the context within which they work. A central characteristic of action research is that it is an interactive process that seeks to understand how and why certain practices work (or do not work). A core feature of action research is its cyclical nature (see Figure 9.1). As there is active gathering of data it is an empirical form of research. The purpose of action research is to create knowledge, even if it is in a limited way, and to then share that knowledge with others (perhaps through collaborative action research, or simply by reporting the results of single research instances).

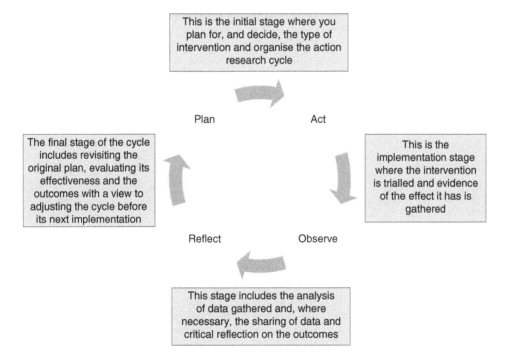

Figure 9.1   The basic action research cycle

Ideally, action research needs to be more than a simple, yet disciplined form of organised self-reflection. The purpose of any research is to inform and initiate what should be some form of transformative change. Action research has the potential to do this and could, it may be argued, be better placed than simply asking people to read research and, as a result of their reading, initiate some form of transformative change to their everyday practice. Reading large-scale research that happened 'elsewhere', in very different contexts, can leave you as the reader feeling that the research findings are not addressing the situation in which you find yourself. Action research – being very personal – immediately provides a context and relevance that are meaningful. Change as a result of action research will therefore have a greater chance of initiating transformative changes in practice. Table 9.2 outlines some of the different types of action research.

Table 9.2   Types of action research (adapted from Ferrance, 2000)

	Individual Research	**Collaborative Research**	**School-wide Research**	**'Regional*' Research**
Focus	Contained within a single classroom – the focus may be an issue or intervention	Carried out across several classrooms, may be a single issue or intervention, often a common issue/intervention	Whole school issue or an agreed area of collective interest	Often an organisational issue or major intervention across several schools
Possible support required	Mentoring or coaching from a more experienced researcher Access to appropriate research materials/databases Advice on data gathering, organisation and analysis techniques	Teacher release for 'fieldwork' Administrative support for managing data, wider reading and centralised access for all researchers	Whole school commitment to the aims and methods used in the research Leadership support which may include release of funding Communication with possible external partners	'Regional' support (e.g. Local Authority, MAT or Federation etc.) Research co-ordinator and/or lead researcher Communication with and involvement of external partners (e.g. local university)
Potential impact	Small-scale changes to local lessons, schemes of work or curriculum Changes to pedagogy Changes to assessment of learners	Changes to schemes of work and school curriculum More widespread changes to pedagogy, though often located within subjects at secondary schools More widespread changes to assessment of learners	Major curriculum change Review of school policies and subsequent changes Wider scale evaluation of structures and school organisation	Redistribution and/or allocation of central resources Development of new Continuing Professional Development programmes for staff Major policy change affecting all schools/institutions Changes to overall organisational structures

	Individual Research	Collaborative Research	School-wide Research	'Regional*' Research
Potential side effects	Teacher pedagogy and professional practice are heavily informed by small datasets Information and results often not shared widely	Improved collegiality Sharing of good practice Formation of group and school-wide partnerships	Improved collegiality	Improved collegiality

*Since the demise of Local Authorities as the main regional support mechanisms for schools, the term 'regional' is being used to denote groups of schools either geographically linked or linked through other mechanisms such as Multi-Academy Trusts (MATS), or serving as maintained schools within a local education authority.

Benefits and drawbacks of small-scale research

Small-scale research such as action research carried out by an individual has the benefit of being directly related to that individual's practice. It will be exactly the right context and it will address the researcher's main concerns and key questions. As such, it can be a very powerful form of research. Those same characteristics, however, are also some of the key weaknesses of small-scale research. If it is 'too' particular, has a small sample of participants or dataset or is very specific to a very particular context, it may well fail to be able to be replicated or applied more widely. In reporting the outcomes of any small-scale research care must be taken to ensure that sweeping claims or generalisations are not made.

The ethics of research and working with children and young adults

The British Educational Research Association (BERA) publishes and encourages high-quality educational research. One of its core aims is to promote a culture of research and improve the practice of academic research for the benefit of society as a whole. The association, which was founded in 1974, publishes internationally renowned academic journals and reviews of education. One very important document for all education researchers is the BERA 'Ethical Guidelines for Educational Research'. The guidelines set out the standards that should be adhered to by researchers in education to ensure that the highest ethical standards are maintained in any context (BERA, 2018).

The guidelines are a comprehensive set of principles about how to ethically carry out research involving children, young adults and vulnerable people. In designing any form of research, these principles must be adhered to and kept in mind. There are five areas of responsibility that any researcher must consider when designing their research project: a responsibility to the participants; a responsibility to sponsors (of the research), clients and other stakeholders in the research; a responsibility to the community of educational researchers; responsibilities surrounding publication and the dissemination of research; and finally, responsibility for the researcher's own well-being and development (BERA, 2018 p.5). Underlying the guidelines is a set of agreed ethical principles, produced by the Academy of Social Sciences (AcSS). These principles are that education research should:

- be inclusive of different interests, values, funders, methods and perspectives;
- respect the privacy, autonomy, diversity, values and dignity of individuals, groups and communities;
- be conducted with integrity throughout, employing the most appropriate methods for research purposes;
- act with regard to the researchers' social responsibilities in conducting and disseminating their research;
- aim to maximise benefit and minimise harm (BERA, 2018 p.4).

BOX 9.1 IS IT ETHICAL?

In applying the principles above, researchers – even those doing small-scale, 'in-house' research in their places of work – must carefully think through the implications of any actions being taken. For example, a planned intervention may be thought to be very beneficial. If this is the case, designing a controlled experiment where the intervention is withheld from one group of children so that an 'effect' could be measured may be viewed as unethical. On what basis are you denying one group of children a potentially beneficial intervention?

Informed consent

Consent, and particularly informed consent, is an issue in education research. Children are not normally considered able to give informed consent, so educational research usually involves gaining such consent from the children's parents or guardians. Where there are vulnerable children, children in care or children with special educational needs or disabilities, access to such children will be very closely guarded, and gaining consent to carry out research will be more difficult.

There are also issues of context that need to be taken into consideration. Where individuals form part of a defined community, the informed consent of the parents may only be one level of consent that needs to be gained.

In some cultures and religions, the community may well have elders or other 'gate-keepers' who may need to provide consent via the parents or guardians.

Informed consent will very much depend on the level and quality of explanation given to those asked for consent. The more open and transparent the explanation of the research is, and the more detail given about the aims, methods etc. being used, the better. For example, what data are being gathered, for what purpose, where will they be held, for how long, whether or not identifiable information will be disguised or removed, and what their rights are with respect to withdrawing from the study or research project, will need to be explained clearly and simply. People will also need to know what will happen to their 'data', i.e. all the information you collect, how it will be analysed and reported, and where you plan to publish your results.

Anonymity

Anonymity is also very important. Counterintuitively, some people are very happy to have their details known and published, and this may include personal details such as age, sex, gender, sexual orientation, and even personal measurements. As researchers, this does not mean that automatically we should use these details, even if consent is given. While anonymity may not always be essential for a research project, it is good practice to always use pseudonyms for people, places, schools etc. The issue of anonymity brings with it aspects of confidentiality and safeguarding. When research evidence includes visual data, care needs to be taken to ensure that any identifying features of individuals or places (e.g. locations, street names, school logos, teacher names, even number plates in the car park just outside the classroom window) are not included. This will ensure that confidentiality is maintained and that safeguarding has been observed. In research, confidentiality extends to not revealing or connecting pseudonyms with real names, and keeping the number of people privy to such information limited.

Some research studies will offer participants payment or some other incentive for taking part. This also raises ethical questions when it comes to education research. Generally, offering a payment as an inducement to take part in research could be considered as introducing a form of bias, i.e. the incentive to provide certain answers to questions could be influenced by the payment or gift. For example, surveying children's likes/dislikes of certain sweets and chocolates would not be helped if those taking part were offered a particular brand of chocolate as a reward. Offering more bars of chocolate depending on the volume of answers given would also be unethical (I should add here that this is purely hypothetical – I have never seen such a piece of research proposed or published).

Summary

Teaching is clearly more than 'just a job'. To be a professional you need to know not only what to do but also why you do it. You need to understand the theoretical basis for the approaches you take, and the practice of reading and applying research is critical to the development of the profession. Sometimes the research we read can seem far away from the actuality of dealing with a classroom of children day after day. Reading about the latest ideas on subjects such as 'cognitive load' or mindset may also raise questions of validity. What is the evidence for these concepts? How rigorous are the studies and do they match 'real life'? We know that over the years many fads have entered teaching – ideas such as 'learning styles' have no empirical research to back them, yet they are seductive as they appear to be intuitive. Before any research enters the day-to-day pedagogy of mainstream teachers we should have a body of evidence to back up those ideas that we can trust. This is part of what being professional means – that you have the skills, expertise and ability to assess research and understand what works and what does not.

In this chapter we explored the idea of professionalism. Expert knowledge, autonomy and professional standards are all part of being professional. Carrying out your own research, i.e. being a competent research practitioner, is also part of being professional. It is the act of being knowledgeably reflective and able to carry out research to enable transformative change in your setting. Action research is one of the most common forms of small-scale research carried out by practising teachers. It's a way of ascertaining 'what works', but that in itself may not be enough – simply planning and carrying out an intervention and recording how pupils perform can often provide evidence of change. It is far too easy then to say that 'this works': ideally any intervention should not only 'work', but also continue to work, and what we are looking for in education is 'what carries on working'.

Any research that is carried out in settings that involve children, young adults or vulnerable people must follow a strict set of ethical guidelines. Even small-scale research carried out by one teacher, in a single classroom, is not exempt from this. Safeguarding and ethical behaviour are paramount, and this should be borne in mind. Gaining informed consent with clear information about what the research is, what it is for, how it will be carried out and reported on, with appropriate safeguards for any data and personal details gathered, is key. Having clear, unambiguous options for participation, non-participation and withdrawal from the research is also vital.

Further reading

British Educational Research Association (BERA) (2018) *Ethical Guidelines for Educational Research* London: BERA

This is the main set of guidelines that all education researchers adhere to when proposing or carring out any form of education research. It is a clear set of guidelines that is accessible and easy to read.

Ferrance, E. (2000) *Action Research* Providence, RI: Northeast and Islands Regional Educational Laboratory, Brown University

This is a very accessible booklet from Brown University that sets out the characteristics and history of action research.

Guerriero, S., & Révai, N. (2017) Knowledge-based teaching and the evolution of a profession. In Guerriero (ed.) *Pedagogical Knowledge and the Changing Nature of the Teaching Profession* pp.253–269 Paris: OECD

This is a chapter from an OECD book on teacher knowledge and professionalism. It looks in depth at what 'being professional' means for teachers.

Bibliography

British Educational Research Association (BERA) (2018) Ethical Guidelines for Educational Research. [online] British Educational Research Association. Available at: www.bera.ac.uk/researchers-resources/publications/ethical-guidelines-for-educational-research-2011 (accessed September 23rd 2017).

Clark-Wilson, A. (2008) Teachers researching their own practice: evidencing student learning using TI-Nspire. In *Proceedings of the Day Conference of the British Society for Research into Learning of Mathematics* Vol. 28 No.2 pp. 7–12 BSRLM, University of Southampton

Darling-Hammond, L. (2005) Teaching as a profession: lessons in teacher preparation and professional development *The Phi Delta Kappan* Vol.87 No,3 pp.237–240

Ferrance, E. (2000) *Action Research*. Providence, RI: Northeast and Islands Regional Educational Laboratory, Brown University.

Hargreaves, L. (2009) The status and prestige of teachers and teaching. In Lawrence, S. & Dworkin, A.G. (eds) *The International Handbook of Research on Teachers and Teaching* pp.217–229 Dordrecht: Springer

Howsam, R.B. (1985) *Educating a Profession* Reprint with Postscript 1985. Report of the Bicentennial Commission on Education for the Profession of Teaching of the American Association of Colleges for Teacher Education

Price, H.E., & Weatherby, K. (2018) The global teaching profession: how treating teachers as knowledge workers improves the esteem of the teaching profession *School Effectiveness and School Improvement* Vol.29 No.1 pp.113–149

Sexton, M. (2007) Evaluating teaching as a profession: implications of a research study for the work of the Teaching Council *Irish Educational Studies* Vol.26 No.1 pp.79–105

Index

Page numbers in *italics* refer to figures; page numbers in **bold** refer to tables.